CLASSIC R̶E̶P̶R̶I̶N̶T̶

RANGERS' EVENTFUL YEARS 1934 to 1951

by John Allan

SOCCER BOOKS LIMITED

FOREWORD

This book was originally published in 1951 in hardback format and copies are now almost impossible to find.

We have therefore decided to produce a new edition as part of our "Classic Reprint" series, to make this scarce title available to the many fans of the Gers who would otherwise be unable to possess a copy.

Details of other titles in our "Classic Reprint" series can be found on the back cover of this book.

British Library Cataloguing in Publication Data
A catalogue record for this book is available from the British Library

ISBN: 978-1-86223-440-6

Copyright © 2020, SOCCER BOOKS LIMITED

72 St. Peter's Avenue, Cleethorpes, N.E. Lincolnshire,
DN35 8HU, United Kingdom
Telephone   01472 696226

Web site   www.soccer-books.co.uk
e-mail   info@soccer-books.co.uk

Printed in the UK by 4edge Ltd.

RANGERS' EVENTFUL YEARS

1934—1951

By JOHN ALLAN

GLASGOW
THE RANGERS FOOTBALL CLUB, LIMITED
IBROX PARK

BOARD OF DIRECTORS.

Standing—William Struth, J.P. (*Manager and Vice-Chairman*); J. Rogers Simpson (*Secretary*).

Sitting—A. L. Morton; W. Gordon Bennett, M.P.; Councillor John F. Wilson, D.L., J.P. (*Chairman*); G. C. P. Brown, M.A.

Mr. W. Gordon Bennett resigned from the Board on Tuesday, 4th September, 1951.

FOREWORD

BY

WILLIAM STRUTH, Director-Manager.

IT is with very great pleasure that I respond to the request to contribute a brief foreword to this little volume which, I feel confident, will be welcomed by every well-wisher of the Rangers' Club.

In the 78 years which have passed since a modest, unheralded birth, Rangers have built up a tradition of which the young, enthusiastic founders would have been very proud. Their successors, it is but fair to say, have reason to feel they have not betrayed the pioneers.

Long before the privilege of managership was conferred on me in June, 1920, Rangers had become an honoured name, not only in Scotland, but in the world of International football.

The years which have followed have been eventful years, marked by varied shades of fortune—high achievement, some disappointment, but always a tenacity of purpose and the ability to take a buffeting and come back full of fight.

I recall, with sincere gratitude to all with whom I have been associated that, since my inauguration as Manager, Rangers' successes have done something to enhance the good name of the Club. These successes have included nine Scottish Cup triumphs, seventeen League Championships, the winning of the Glasgow Cup on eighteen occasions, and the Charity Cup twenty times.

In the pages which follow, you will read of other accomplishments by men who have worn our colours, and I think you will agree that the narrative has been told with commendable fairness to all concerned.

William Struth

A3

THE REASON.

WHEN first " The Story of the Rangers " was written, followed by " Eleven Great Years," no further sequel was envisaged. Since 1934, however, requests have been received from friends abroad and from Rangers followers at home, for a record of events which would bring up to date the varied fortunes of the club.

As many wellwishers were unable to procure a copy of the two previous volumes, it has been considered helpful to embrace in the present one some details which summarise the achievements of the men who have worn the colours since the Rangers club was formed 78 years ago.

But, mainly, the purpose is to chronicle what has happened since the " Eleven Great Years " was issued and, indeed, much that is worth telling remains to be told.

Up to the end of season 1950 - 51, Rangers have played in :—

22 Scottish Cup Finals,	-	- Won	13
42 Glasgow Cup Finals,	-	- ,,	31
45 Charity Cup Finals,	-	- ,,	28

Scottish Cup Finals include those of 1878-79 when, after a draw with Vale of Leven, Rangers' claim to have won was disallowed and they did not replay ; and the Final of 1908 - 09, when the Cup was withheld.

Owing to World War II, the Scottish Cup was competed for in only ten of the seventeen seasons from 1934 - 35 till 1950 - 51. In these ten seasons, Rangers contested five Finals and won them all.

In the ten seasons since 1933 - 34 in which the Scottish League was in operation, Rangers were six times champions. The Southern League, a war-time competition, was won by Rangers in each of its six seasons. The Southern League Cup, which took the place of the Scottish Cup, was won four times.

In 1946, a Victory Cup was competed for and Rangers won it.

Rangers have been 27 times champions of the Scottish League, including a joint championship with Dumbarton in the first season of the competition. In season 1904 - 05, they aggregated the same number of points as Celtic and, under the present rule, would have been champions on goal average. A deciding game was played and Celtic won.

Only twice since the Scottish League began have Rangers finished lower than fourth. These figures tell the story :—

Position.						Seasons.
Champions,	-	-	-	-	-	27
Runners-up,	-	-	-	-	-	12
Third,	-	-	-	-	-	10
Fourth,	-	-	-	-	-	3
Fifth, -	-	-	-	-	-	1
Sixth,	-	-	-	-	-	1

To official representative matches, Rangers have provided a greater number of players than any club in Britain. Against the home countries, the figures of our players honoured up till end of season 1950-51 are as follows :—

England, -	-	-	151	Irish League, -	-	76
Wales, -	-	-	135	League of Ireland,		9
Ireland, -	-	-	141			
English League,	-	177				689

AGAINST OTHER COUNTRIES.

France, -	-	-	18	Switzerland,	-	6
Austria, -	-	-	11	Holland, -	-	3
Czechoslovakia,	-	6	Hungary, -	-	2
Belgium,	-	-	10	Luxembourg	-	3
Germany,	-	-	4			
Denmark,	-	-	4			70
Portugal,	-	-	3			

Grand Aggregate,   759

These are the figures which tell their own story.

CONTENTS.

		PAGE
Foreword,	.. ..	5
Season 1934 - 35,	.. ..	11
Cup and League Won,	.. ..	12
Season 1935 - 36,	.. ..	14
Scottish Cup Conquest,	.. ..	14
Two Stalwarts' Farewell,	.. ..	16
Alex. Venter's Record,	.. ..	19
Season 1936 - 37,	.. ..	20
League Flag Regained,	.. ..	20
Germans at the Stadium,	.. ..	21
Season 1937 - 38,	.. ..	23
Willie Thornton's Goals,	.. ..	25
George Brown's Honour,	.. ..	26
Season 1938 - 39,	.. ..	27
Jock Shaw Arrives,	.. ..	27
The League Again,	.. ..	28
Stadium Record Attendance,	.. ..	28
Our Games with Arsenal,	.. ..	29
Willie Waddell's Debut,	.. ..	30
War Years,	.. ..	31
Victory Cup Won,	.. ..	32
James Duncanson,	.. ..	33
Willie Woodburn,	.. ..	34
Our Dynamo Clash,	.. ..	35
George Brown's Record,	.. ..	37
Season 1946 - 47,	.. ..	38

Dougie Gray, ... 39

Jamie Smith, ... 39

Sam Cox, ... 41

Bobbie Brown, ... 42

Season 1947 - 48, ... 43

Three Cups Won, ... 43

Final Struggle with Morton, ... 44

Season 1948 - 49, ... 46

A Triple Triumph, ... 46

Dundee's Unlucky Break, ... 46

League Won by a Point, ... 46

Season 1949 - 50, ... 50

Second Scottish Cup Hat-trick, ... 51

The Men Who Did It, ... 52

Hibs' Great League Challenge, ... 53

One Point Again Does It, ... 53

Jock Shaw's Record, ... 55

Season 1950 - 51, ... 56

Trophies Lost, ... 56

George Young's Record, ... 59

Treasured Gifts, ... 62

Rangers' Victory Years, ... 64-65

Scottish Cup Winning Teams, ... 66

History in Figures, ... 67-101

Rangers' Caps, ... 102-105

Analysis of League Results, ... 107-143

Directors—Past and Present, ... 146

LIST OF ILLUSTRATIONS.

PAGE

Board of Directors, - - - - - *facing* 3

They Set the Example, - - - - - ,, 14

Reception Room, - - - - - ,, 15

Ibrox Stadium, 1951, - - - - - ,, 24

Historic Trophies, - - - - - ,, 24, 25

A Notable Feat, - - - - - - ,, 25

New Scottish Cup Triumph, - - - - ,, 32

Where the Trophies reside, - - - - ,, 33

We Value these Trophies, - - - - ,, 48

3-Cup Victors, - - - - - - ,, 52

A Feat Unequalled, - - - - - ,, 53

Our Players, - - - - - - ,, 60

1934—1935.

Cup and League Again—Hearts' Challenge—Acas.
Made it Close—Old Campaigner Gone.

WHEN the story of " Eleven Great Years " closed in 1934, Rangers were in possession of the Scottish Cup, Glasgow Cup and Charity Cup, as well as the Scottish League Championship.

On the balance of chance, and with all the human factors in mind, it was not to be expected that such a notable sequence of successes would soon be repeated, yet what actually was accomplished in this season of 1934 - 35 was sufficiently noteworthy to give all concerned the warmest satisfaction.

The Scottish Cup and the League Championship were won again, and in the Glasgow Cup Final we lost to Partick Thistle by an only goal. Thistle later deprived us of our hold on the Charity Cup, again by an only goal, in the semi-final, and defeating Queen's Park in the final, took the trophy to Firhill to keep company with the Glasgow Cup.

It was a 20-club League. The opposition was exceptionally strong, and we had to approach almost every game as though it were a cup-tie. When Kilmarnock won at Ibrox, in December, it was our first home League defeat in three seasons.

Fortune was kind to us in giving us home ties in the first three rounds of the Scottish Cup, but when the fourth-round draw sent us to Fir Park, we felt that danger was nigh. However, centre forward Jimmy Smith, who was hitting the target with easy facility all season—he scored 36 League goals—gave us four goals—and we went into the semi-final to face Hearts, for whom Tommy Walker had largely been responsible for taking them thus far.

It took two games at Hampden to settle the tie. Walker scored for Hearts and Torry Gillick for Rangers. Back to Hampden, Bob McPhail gave Rangers a half-time lead, which looked pretty good until Davie Meiklejohn broke down when the second half was twenty minutes gone. He struggled on to the field after attention, but he was hopelessly crippled and had to quit.

It was Hearts' opportunity, but when Bobby Main cracked on a second goal for Rangers, our defence took heart, and Hearts had to accept defeat.

So it was Rangers and Hamilton Academicals for the Final, and here is how they lined up at Hampden before about 90,000 spectators :—

> **Rangers.**—Dawson ; Gray and McDonald ; Kennedy, Simpson and Brown ; Main, Venters, Smith, McPhail and Gillick.

> **Hamilton Academicals.**—Morgan ; Wallace and Bulloch ; Cox, McStay and Murray ; King, McLaren, Wilson, Harrison and Reid.

Academicals were a tightly-knit side, who could finish fourth in the League. They demanded complete respect, and they proved worthy Finalists. It was a keenly-contested match, but we pulled through with two more goals by Jimmy Smith, against one by Bert Harrison for the Academicals.

We had won the Cup and the League for the second season in succession. Almost as pleasing was our victory at Ibrox against the Sportklub Rapide team from Austria, which, with certain changes, had surprised the world two seasons previously by their brilliant display against us in a drawn match.

That game revealed to all who doubted—there were many—that the Continentals had now seriously to be reckoned with.

We cannot close this chapter without recalling that in November, 1935, our grand old campaigner, Sandy

Archibald, was transferred back to Raith Rovers. No player ever held a warmer corner in the hearts of Rangers' officials and followers. At home and on tour abroad, Sandy was ever the jolly companion. As fine a tribute ever paid him was that by Willie Maley, when manager of Celtic, who said, " We can never be sure of beating Rangers when Sandy Archibald is on the field." Mr. Maley had reason for saying so.

Sandy was manager of Dunfermline at the time of his death, which was regretted in all football circles.

We had to surrender our hold on the Glasgow Cup and the Charity Cup, both of which were won by Partick Thistle, to whom we fell victims, each time by an only goal, in the Final of the Glasgow Cup and in the Semi-final of the Charity Cup, as has been earlier stated.

Thistle's Charity Cup success was specially noteworthy, as on the day of the Final, against Queen's Park, three of their players—Cummings, Donnelly and Miller—were on their way to America with a Scottish touring team.

Jimmy Simpson captained the Scottish team which defeated England at Hampden, and he had George Brown and Bob McPhail in support.

1934-35.

League Champions.

Scottish Cup.		Glasgow Cup.		Charity Cup.	
Cowdenbeath (H),	3–1	Celtic (A),	2–1	Third Lanark	
Third Lanark (H),	2–0	Partick Thistle		(H),	3–1
St. Mirren (H),	1–0	(Hampden), 0–1		Partick Thistle	
Motherwell (A),	4–1			(A),	0–1
Hearts (Hampden),	1–1				
Hearts (Hampden),	2–0				
Hamilton Acas. (Hampden),	2–1				

v. England.	v. Wales.	v. Ireland.	v. English League.
J. Simpson.	J. Simpson.	J. Dawson.	J. Simpson.
G. C. P. Brown.	G. C. P. Brown.	J. Simpson.	R. Main.
R. McPhail.		J. Smith.	

13

1935—1936

The   Cup   Retained—Stern   Pittodrie   Tussle—
Doughty Third Lanark—Two Rangers' Stalwarts.

HAVING won the Scottish Cup twice in succession,
and the League Championship in the previous
three seasons, there was a pardonable feeling of
optimism when we embarked on the new campaign.

Our objectives were akin to those of our rivals,
and it was only as events unfolded that we began to realise
the possibility of creating a little bit of football history,
which we had not dared to put into tangible shape as part
of our ambition.

Without the loss of a goal, we brought the Glasgow Cup
back to Ibrox, but previous to defeating Celtic in the
Final, with goals by Jimmy Fiddes and Torry Gillick, we
had played strenuous " prestige " games, home and away,
with Sheffield Wednesday, English Cup holders, and a
home match with Arsenal, English League champions.

We would not hold these contests wholly responsible for
the loss of valuable League points which closely followed,
but it is reasonable to suppose that the players felt the
strain, and that, under other circumstances, points lost
would have been gained, and so have had a bearing on the
ultimate championship decision.

Our first League reverse was inflicted by Celtic, at Ibrox,
notable because it was their first points victory at the
Stadium since 1921, and this was 1935. We squared the
account at Parkhead on New Year's Day, in a match
which was remarkable for the fact that, for long after-
wards, many who were present argued about the half-time
score.

14

THEY SET THE EXAMPLE.

In season 1935-36, Rangers completed the winning of the Scottish Cup in three successive seasons, an achievement since repeated. In the photograph are the players who took part in the third of the three competitions. (*See page 17*).

Back Row—J. Dawson, J. Smith, J. Wallace, D. Wallace, J. Simpson, J. Drysdale, W. A. Cheyne, R. Campbell. W. Thornton, G. Jenkins

Second Row—W. Struth (*Manager*), J. Stewart, R. McPhail, J. Galloway, T. Soutar, T. McKillop, J. Reid, G. McKenzie, J. Fiddes, J. Turnbull, R. McDonald, A. Dixon (*Trainer*)

Front Row—J. Kennedy, D. Gray, D. McLatchie, A. Venters, T. Hart, D. Meiklejohn (*Captain*), R. Main, G. Brown, D. Kinnear, A. Winning, A. Macaulay.

RECEPTION ROOM.

A section of the reception room at the Stadium, much admired by visitors from England and the Continent.

In the excitement which prevailed, a goal scored by Bob McPhail, just as the interval whistle sounded, passed unnoticed by numbers of spectators. Up till then, Celtic had looked like winning by a big handful of goals, but Rangers turned the game completely round in the second half and won 4 – 3, thanks greatly to skilful strategy by Davie Meiklejohn, ably abetted by Bob McPhail.

Rangers lost only two of the last 16 League games, but these defeats, and an unexpected home draw with Motherwell, were sufficient to deprive us of the championship, which was worthily taken by Celtic for the first time in ten seasons.

However, that little bit of history, to which earlier reference has been made, had yet to come. We were to capture the Scottish Cup for the third time in succession, a feat never before accomplished since pre-professional days, when conditions bore no comparison with those now existing.

To win the Scottish Cup, luck, even a little of it, will often play a vital part. In that connection, the draw was once again kind to us until the fourth round sent us to Pittodrie.

Aberdeen had beaten us in the League there, and they beat us again at Ibrox after we had won the Cup. They finished equal with us on points, and were, in fact, a team capable of anything, so that we realised that a victory for us at Pittodrie would virtually mean the Cup for Ibrox again, especially as Celtic—League champions—had gone out beaten in the second round by St. Johnstone, at Parkhead.

Well, the Pittodrie tie fulfilled all our expectations. It was a desperately fought tussle, watched by what was a ground record crowd up till then.

Forwards on neither side could make any decisive impression on the defence, and a draw seemed the certain, and fairest, result when Rangers' outside left, Jimmy Turnbull, went romping down the wing to finish with a scoring shot which won the tie.

Clyde, in the semi-final, did not give much trouble, but Third Lanark proved formidable Finalists. The line-up was :—

> **Rangers.**—Dawson ; Gray and Cheyne ; Meiklejohn, Simpson and Brown ; Fiddes, Venters, Smith, McPhail and Turnbull.

> **Third Lanark.**—Muir ; Carabine and Hamilton ; Blair, Denmark and McInnes ; Howe, Gallacher, Hay, Kennedy and Kinnaird.

That was a good Third Lanark eleven, so good that it required one of Jerry Dawson's finest displays of goalkeeping to pull us through with a Bob McPhail goal. Third's left back was our old colleague, " Newry " Hamilton, who had won two Scottish Cup medals with us, and he played a real man's part in keeping the result in suspense until the last whistle.

This was Bob McPhail's sixth Scottish Cup medal won with Rangers, to which had to be added his first, gained with Airdrieonians, to make seven in all. His other awards were—seven Glasgow Cup medals, eight Charity Cup, and nine League championship.

He was capped 13 times, five times against England, and he played for the Scottish League five times against the English League. Injury prevented his honours being augmented.

His first eleven competition games for Rangers, and goals scored, are here summarised :—

R. McPHAIL.

	Matches.	Goals.		Matches.	Goals.
1926-27, -	3	4	1933-34, -	35	25
1927-28, -	45	25	1934-35, -	41	15
1928-29, -	41	21	1935-36, -	36	26
1929-30, -	35	19	1936-37, -	38	31
1930-31, -	41	23	1937-38, -	32	13
1931-32, -	49	29	1938-39, -	27	15
1932-33, -	38	33	1939-40, -	5	2
	Matches, 466.			**Goals, 281.**	

On 22nd April, 1936, Davie Meiklejohn, who had worn Rangers' colours for 17 years, played his last League match, which was against Hearts, at Ibrox. He had captained Rangers and Scotland, won close on 50 medals, Juvenile, Junior and Senior, represented Scotland in 14 Internationals, and played for the Scottish League against the English League five times. His six Scottish Cup medals fell short by one of the record held jointly by Bob McPhail and Jimmy McMenemy, Celtic (6) and Partick Thistle (1).

Matches and goals for Rangers:

D. MEIKLEJOHN.

	Matches.	Goals.			Matches.	Goals.
1919-20, -	14	2	1928-29, -		39	5
1920-21, -	46	5	1929-30, -		46	1
1921-22, -	45	5	1930-31, -		37	2
1922-23, -	40	1	1931-32, -		47	5
1923-24, -	45	8	1932-33, -		37	2
1924-25, -	46	5	1933-34, -		38	2
1925-26, -	12	0	1934-35, -		27	3
1926-27, -	37	2	1935-36, -		36	4
1927-28, -	43	2				
Matches, 635.			**Goals, 54.**			

Rangers had accomplished what many well-wishers considered the impossible. The Scottish Cup was won for the third season in succession, and the club's official handbook said the performance would probably never be equalled.

It was equalled, as we shall see, and by none other than Rangers themselves. Players who contributed to the

17

B

three-Cup triumphs and the number of games played in
the ties :—

THE THREE CUP VICTORS.

	1933-34.	1934-35.	1935-36.	Total.
J. Dawson, -	6	7	6	19
D. Gray, -	7	7	6	20
R. McDonald,	6	7	2	15
D. Meiklejohn,	5	3	6	14
J. Simpson, -	7	7	6	20
G. Brown, -	6	7	6	19
T. Craig, -	3	..	..	3
J. Marshall, -	7	..	..	7
J. Smith, -	6	6	6	18
R. McPhail, -	6	7	6	19
J. Fleming, -	5	..	..	5
T. Hamilton, -	1	..	..	1
T. Russell, -	1	..	..	1
R. Main, -	6	6	1	13
A. Macaulay, -	1	..	..	1
W. G. Nicholson,	3	..	..	3
A. Venters, -	1	7	6	14
J. Kennedy, -	..	2	..	2
T. Gillick, -	..	7	..	7
S. Roberts, -	..	3	..	3
W. Hay, -	..	1	..	1
W. A. Cheyne,	..	..	4	4
J. Turnbull, -	..	..	6	6
J. Fiddes, -	..	..	5	5
	77	77	66	220

1935-36.

Scottish Cup.		Glasgow Cup.		Charity Cup.	
East Fife (H),	3–1	Queen's Park		Third Lanark	
Albion Rovers (A),	3–1	(H),	2–0	(H),	1–0
St. Mirren (A),	2–1	Clyde (H),	2–0	Clyde (A),	1 0
Aberdeen (A),	1–0	Celtic (H),	2–0	Celtic	
Clyde (Hampden),	3–0			(Hampden),	2–4
Third Lanark					
(Hampden),	1–0				

v. England.	v. Wales.	v. Ireland.	v. English League.	v. Irish League.
J. Dawson	J Simpson.	J. Simpson.	J Dawson.	J Dawson.
J. Simpson	G C P. Brown.		J. Simpson.	J. Simpson
G. C. P Brown.			G C P. Brown.	
A. Venters			R. Main.	
			A. Venters.	

In home-and-away games with Sheffield Wednesday, English Cup winners, Rangers drew 1–1, at Sheffield, and won 2–0, at Ibrox. A draw, 2–2, resulted from a match at Ibrox, with Arsenal, English League champions.

By this time, Alec Venters, who had come from Cowdenbeath in November, 1933, had qualified as a first-team unit. He had felt strange to the new atmosphere at first and, in fact, had expressed to Manager Struth his doubts about ever making the grade. " Carry on," said the manager, " we'll tell you if we're not pleased." The Cowdenbeath laddie " carried on," got two Scottish Cup medals, helped to win four League Championships, and received the highest International honours. His service to Rangers will stand inspection.

ALEX. VENTERS.

	Matches.	Goals.		Matches.	Goals.
1933-34, -	15	7	1940-41, -	37	15
1934-35, -	37	10	1941-42, -	26	18
1935-36, -	43	17	1942-43, -	4	3
1936-37, -	39	11	1943-44, -	4	3
1937-38, -	44	18	1944-45, -	24	20
1938-39, -	38	28	1945-46, -	5	3
1939-40, -	39	21			

Matches, 396.	Goals, 188.

1936—1937

EVERY season has its own distinctive features, some good, some not so good. In this one we could recover the championship in a 20-club League. Only two teams beat us, Hearts twice, and Clyde, at Shawfield.

We won the Glasgow Cup for the 23rd time, defeating Celtic in the semi-final after sharing League points with them at Parkhead, while, at Ibrox, on New Year's Day, we collected both points before a then record attendance of 95,000.

These results with our old Parkhead rivals are mentioned to indicate the contrasts which can arise as between club and club, for while Celtic went on to win the Scottish Cup, we, the holders, made our departure from the competition in the first round at Palmerston, where an only goal scored by Queen of the South centre forward, John Renwick, did the damage.

This Palmerston game was typical of several. Too often the forward line failed to function, although Jimmy Smith, with 31 League goals, and Bob McPhail with 25, contributed greatly to our championship success. Trouble was that we too often drew a blank.

When we met the Arsenal at Highbury, we suffered our only defeat in our five games with them and, here again, our forward line, weakened by injuries, it must be said, failed to rise to the occasion.

As we had opened the season with a 4 - 1 victory against Austria F.C., we had felt that it was to be a season right up to the acknowledged Rangers' standard.

Perhaps the fault of creating an exceptional standard is that you are expected to maintain it, and those who have tried to do so know of the hazards that lie in wait.

In the first half of the season, Scotland gained what, at the time, was looked upon as an important victory against a strong German eleven, at Ibrox, and Rangers players who assisted were Jerry Dawson, Jimmy Simpson (captain), George Brown and Bob McPhail.

During the previous close season, Archie Macaulay, who had been with us since 1933, was transferred to West Ham United, and later played for Brentford and Arsenal, with whom he was "capped" against England, Wales and Ireland, in addition to playing against France, Switzerland and Belgium. His success in the International sphere was followed with warm appreciation by Rangers' officials and supporters.

Along with the International caps awarded Rangers' players, centre half Jimmy Simpson was chosen captain against England, Wales and Ireland, while left half George Brown, led out the Scots against the English League and Irish League.

In the case of Jock Shaw, events merely cast their shadows before : he was left back against the English League, but he was of Airdrieonians, as yet.

So perhaps it wasn't such a bad season after all. We were free, and pleased, to compliment Aberdeen on the run they had given us for the championship. At one stage, they held what appeared to be an unassailable lead, but the strain of going for the Scottish Cup, as well, told upon them. They were good runners-up, and though they were beaten in the Cup Final, they lived to fight and win another day ; their Cup triumph came in 1946-47 when they defeated Hibernian in the Final.

1936-37.

League Champions.

Scottish Cup.		Glasgow Cup.		Charity Cup.	
Queen of the South (A),	0—1	Queen's Park (H), 4—1 Celtic (H), 2—1 Partick Thistle (H), 2—2 Partick Thistle (H), 6—1		Queen's Park (H),	0—3

v. England.	*v.* Wales.	*v.* Ireland.	*v.* English League.	*v* Irish League.
J. Dawson. J. Simpson. G. C P Brown. R. McPhail.	J. Dawson. J. Simpson. G. C P. Brown	J. Dawson J Simpson G C P. Brown	J. Dawson. G C.P Brown R. McPhail D Kinnear	J Dawson W. A Cheyne. G. C P Brown

Every possible award was conferred on Jerry Dawson and George Brown and, to help on the good work, Bob McPhail scored two of Scotland's three goals against England at Hampden.

1937—1938

League Lapses—So Near the Cup !—A Foolish
Penalty—Glasgow Cup Held—Willie Thornton's
Goals.

FOR a team going through a certain process of
transition, season 1937-38 was, in one respect,
not altogether unsatisfactory. The disappointing
feature was that, having gone so far in the major competitions, we stopped short of supreme achievement.

To finish third in the League behind Celtic and Hearts
was not, in itself, a performance calling for criticism, but,
analysed, the record showed far too many blemishes—and
the loyal supporter is no mean analyst.

When the semi-final of the Scottish Cup was reached,
hopes of the trophy being brought back to Ibrox after a
year's absence appeared to be justified.

Kilmarnock, who had qualified to meet us at Hampden,
had been having a desperate struggle to ward off relegation
and, in fact, finished only a point above Dundee, who went
down along with Morton.

But Killie had shown that they could rise to an occasion
when they defeated Celtic, the cup-holders, at Parkhead,
in the third round, an event which ranked as the season's
biggest sensation since Celtic, in the Parkhead League
fixture, had trounced Killie to the extent of 8–0.

For Rangers, however, the semi-final was an ill-starred
affair. Well on in the second half we looked to
have the match won, but when our defence foolishly gave
away a penalty, which cost us a goal, Kilmarnock took a
new lease of life.

Our players, on the contrary, became more than a little
worried and, as so often happens in such circumstances,

23

the side that had appeared set for victory took a knock-out blow in the last minute when Killie got a fourth and winning goal.

For us the Final had only a sentimental interest. Kilmarnock proved true to type, made a brave stand against a well-balanced East Fife team which, winning in extra time after the first game had been drawn, became the only Second Division club ever to win the Scottish Cup.

As offset against the disappointment, the Glasgow Cup was won for the third season in succession, but in the Final of the Charity Cup, Celtic, whom we had defeated in the semi-final of the Glasgow, took their revenge.

Our reserves were good enough to win the Scottish Second Eleven Cup, making the sixteenth occasion on which the trophy had been brought to the Stadium.

Another event which must be narrated was our match with Stoke City, the sequel to which is perpetuated at each Ne'erday in the reception room at Ibrox.

Stoke manager, Bob McGrory, was commissioned by the civic heads of the town to come to Glasgow and ask Rangers to play a match on behalf of the sufferers from the Markham Colliery Disaster. Rangers had already been obliged to cancel a game with Arsenal because of pressure of fixtures but, in view of the purpose for which the match with Stoke City was suggested, they gladly agreed to the request.

As a result of the match, close on £2,000 was added to the Disaster Fund. In the evening, the Rangers' players and officials were fêted in the City Hall, when Sir Francis Joseph, President of the Stoke Club, who presided, presented Rangers with a Loving Cup made from his own special mould.

Sir Francis requested that on the occasion of the first match played at Ibrox in each New Year, the Loving Cup be brought out and the Stoke game suitably commemorated.

THE STADIUM AS IT IS TO-DAY.

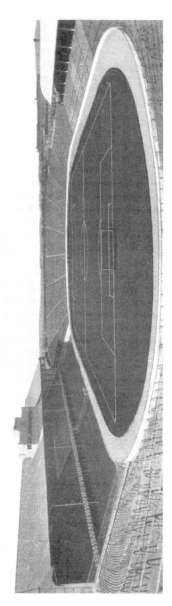

During the close season of 1951, the pitch was re-turfed at an approximate cost of £15,000. Now it is considered one of the finest playing surfaces in Britain.

When the photograph was taken in 1947, Rangers were in possession of the Victory Cup, Glasgow Cup, Charity Cup and the League Championship Cup. All the other trophies in the photograph are the club's own property (Victory Cup included), either won in contest or presented to them.

1 Glasgow Cup.

2 North-Eastern Supplementary Cup.

3 Presented by the Rapid Club in Vienna

4 Victory Cup

5. Another trophy presented by Rapid Club

6 Replica of Southern League Cup presented to out players.

7 Scottish League Cup

8. Presented by the Czechs when they played at Ibrox.

9. Scottish League Championship Cup.

10 Summer Cup.

11. Glasgow Charity Cup.

12 Sinclair Trophy won in match against R A F.

13 Loving Cup presented by Sir Francis Joseph, Chairman of Stoke F.C.

14. Presented by Sir Patrick Dollan when Rangers defeated Preston North End in War Relief Match.

As a tribute to the players who won the Scottish League Championship in three of the first four seasons after the end of the war, a special gold medal was presented to each of them. Jock Shaw was captain and it is his medal which is reproduced along with miniature replicas of the championship flags (*see page* 54).

[*Photo by T. & R. Annan & Sons.*

In the passing years the request has been duly honoured.

In this year of 1937 there came to Ibrox a boy from Winchburgh named Willie Thornton, who stayed to become the long-service Rangers' player of his time.

Not being the professional age of 17, he played some games as an amateur and made his League debut as such, at outside right, against Partick Thistle on 2nd January, 1937. I think most of those looking on saw in him something which would take him far in the game. He did not belie those first impressions.

On " coming of age," he was duly signed as a professional and, over the years, has made for himself a record of performances of which he has good reason to be proud.

But for the war, in which he served for five years, and was awarded the Military Medal for gallantry at the invasion of Sicily, where the fighting was tough, the chances are that he would have come near to the best British scoring records. You can realise that from what this Winchburgh laddie actually accomplished for Rangers in first-eleven matches.

WILLIE THORNTON.

	Matches.	Goals.		Matches.	Goals.
1936-37, -	6	1	1945-46, -	18	10
1937-38, -	20	7	1946-47, -	38	24
1938-39, -	43	23	1947-48, -	51	26
1939-40, -	41	28	1948-49, -	46	36
1940-41, -	7	3	1949-50, -	31	20
1941-42, -	6	2	1950-51, -	34	20
1942-43, -	4	4			
	Matches, 345.		Goals, 204.		

In two seasons, 1943-44 and 1944-45, Army service prevented him from having a single game, while in three other seasons, while the war was on, he had only 17 games in all.

RANGERS' EVENTFUL YEARS

It is to be regretted that no authentic record was kept of his headed goals, but in one season, at least—that was 1948-49—22 of his 36 goals were scored with the head.

Willie Thornton, from the wee village of Winchburgh, will be remembered as one who wore light blue to the honour of himself and the club he served.

1937-38.

Scottish Cup.		Glasgow Cup.		Charity Cup.	
Alloa (A),	6-1	Clyde (A),	3-1	Clyde (H),	4-1
Queen of the South		Celtic (A),	2-1	Third Lanark	
(H),	3-1	Third Lanark		(H),	1-0
A Bye		(Hampden),	2-1	Celtic	
Falkirk (A),	2-1			(Hampden),	0-2
Kilmarnock					
(Hampden),	3-4				

v. England.	v. Wales.	v. Ireland.	v. English League	v Irish League
G. C. P. Brown.	J. Dawson J. Simpson. G. C. P. Brown R Main R. McPhail.	J. Dawson. J. Simpson. J Smith. R McPhail.	J. Dawson A. Venters	J. Dawson.

In addition to these awards, George Brown (as captain) and Jerry Dawson represented Scotland against Czechoslovakia and Holland. David Kinnear played against the Czechs and J. McKillop against Holland.

1938—1939

Fighting Back—New Signings—Another Championship—Scottish Cup Exit—Arsenal Return.

BY this time everyone had come to recognise that a
price had to be paid for the remodelling of a team
whose past attainments had set a target not easy
to approach.

Several of the tried and trusted campaigners were
naturally feeling the effects of long, strenuous service.
Dougie Gray had been thirteen seasons in the top grade of
defenders ; Bob McPhail was only two seasons short of
Dougie's tenure, and had been in the leading class of
forwards, with Airdrieonians, before reaching Ibrox ;
Jimmy Simpson was beginning his twelfth season ; Jimmy
Smith and George Brown their eleventh ; Bob (Whitey)
McDonald, brought from Canada in 1928, also his eleventh.

With such stalwarts nearing the twilight of their playing
career, a formidable task of replacement was presented,
but, though we could not see into the future, we were to
realise, in time, that the arrival at Ibrox, in the close
season of 1938, of Jock (Tiger) Shaw, Willie Waddell,
Scott Symon and Jimmy Duncanson, would greatly assist
in restoring the balance between loss and gain.

Willie Woodburn had preceded them by some seven or
eight months and, as you know, became the established
pivot after George Young, signed three years later, had
moved from centre half to right back.

Prior to the opening of this 1938 - 39 season, we had the
Empire Exhibition Cup played at the Stadium.   Everton,
Sunderland, Chelsea and Brentford took part in a knock-
out competition with Celtic, Aberdeen, Hearts and Rangers.

We were drawn against Everton in the first round, played badly and were beaten 2 - 0, the only extenuating circumstance being that our goalkeeper, Jerry Dawson, was injured 14 minutes after half-time, and took no further part.

Further solatium might have been found in the fact that Everton proved the best team in the competition, though beaten 1 - 0 in the Final by Celtic, in extra time, and after their cleverest forward, inside right Cunliffe, had been injured.

Our trophies won were the League Championship and the Charity Cup, which could not compensate for an undignified dismissal from the Scottish Cup on our own ground. We lost to Clyde, the ultimate Cup winners, and the undeniable reason was that Clyde were the superior team. They were, in fact, a very good team and won the Cup with the loss of only one goal, that was scored from a penalty by our Alec Lyness.

We opened the League programme cheerfully, but when we went to Parkhead for our sixth game and took a 6 - 2 drubbing, the Sunday papers told the world, in big type, the RANGERS WERE ON THE SLIDE.

We won the championship with only four defeats in 38 games, and we had it won before we got our fourth reverse.

So Rangers must have found the secret of " sliding " up instead of down !

Our Parkhead adventure had apparently not been forgotten when Ne'erday came round. Celtic were at our heels, and another win for them, at Ibrox, could have given our championship aspirations a shake. So, 118,561 persons paid to see the show, and it was reckoned that, all told, the attendance reached 120,000. That Ibrox record still stands.

With goals by Alec Venters and David Kinnear, Rangers won against a goal by Celtic's Carruth, and did not lose

28

another League game until Aberdeen beat them **at** Pittodrie, in the closing fixture, the championship, **as** already told, having been previously clinched.

Early in the season we had the pleasure of renewing **our** intercourse with Arsenal, who came to the Stadium **as** English League champions. We won an exciting **tussle** by an only goal, and as it was the last of our **meetings,** soon to be revived, we hope, it may be helpful to give **here** the results of our six engagements :—

1933-34,	-	Ibrox,	Rangers,	**2** ;	Arsenal,	**0**
1933-34,	-	Highbury,	Rangers,	**3** ;	Arsenal,	**1**
1934-35,	-	Highbury,	Arsenal,	**1** ;	Rangers,	**1**
1935-36,	-	Ibrox,	Rangers,	**2** ;	Arsenal,	**2**
1936-37,	-	Highbury,	Arsenal,	**2** ;	Rangers,	**1**
1938-39,	-	Ibrox,	Rangers,	**1** ;	Arsenal,	**0**

1938 - 39.
League Champions.

Scottish Cup.		Glasgow Cup.		Charity Cup.	
Raith Rovers (A),	1–0	Queen's Park		Queen's Park	
Hamilton Acas. (H),	2–0	(A),	0–0	(H),	2–1
Clyde (H),	1–4	Queen's Park		Third Lanark	
		(H),	2 -3	(Hampden),	
				7 corners to 4	
				corners.	

v. England.	*v.* Ireland.	*v* English League.	*v.* Irish League.
J. Dawson A. Venters.	J. Dawson.	A. Venters. D. Kinnear.	J. Dawson.

Jerry Dawson was chosen to play against the **English** League, but had to withdraw, and John Brown **(Clyde)** came in. Dawson and Scott Symon played for **Scotland** against Hungary at Ibrox.

The goal that beat the Arsenal was scored by a boy **who** was making his debut for Rangers' first eleven. He **was**

Willie Waddell, destined for a football career that was to see him go right to the top.

Willie was a schoolboy of 15 when he first pulled a light blue jersey over his sturdy shoulders. His schoolmaster said, "Go ahead," when the pupil sought permission to leave early and make a dash for Firhill to play for Rangers' reserves against Partick Thistle.

Before being called up for more serious business at the Stadium, he was given a breaking-in spell with Strathclyde. Then came his senior debut against Arsenal, on 29th August, 1938.

At Lanark Grammar School he could take a turn in any forward position, for he has what the knowing ones call "two good feet." Though outside right is his favourite position, anyone can see that he loves to have a hearty crack at the ball with his left.

His exceptional turn of speed, allied to natural physical strength, has gained for him the respect of opposing defenders of every grade.

Of England's Ernie Hapgood he says, "The best back I ever played against."

For Rangers' first team, his League and Cup games, and goals scored in these are :—

WILLIE WADDELL.

	Matches.	Goals.		Matches.	Goals.
1938-39, -	33	8	1945-46, -	48	24
1939-40, -	37	8	1946-47, -	29	5
1940-41, -	15	6	1947-48, -	25	3
1941-42, -	22	8	1948-49, -	34	7
1942-43, -	45	13	1949-50, -	22	9
1943-44, -	32	7	1950-51, -	39	8
1944-45, -	41	20			

Matches, 422.	Goals, 126.

In his Internationals he has been specially severe on Wales, against whom he scored in 1945, 1946 and 1948 (two). He got two goals against Ireland in 1949, and one against the Irish League in 1949.

1939—1946

WAR YEARS and VICTORY CUP WON

WHEN Britain declared war on Germany on 3rd September, 1939, the whole face of the game underwent a drastic change. We had immediately to adjust ourselves to the altered conditions, but with the wholehearted approval of highest authority that the game should be kept going as a sedative to the folks who were compelled to live under a strain which called for physical and mental resistance.

Two major competitions, the Scottish League and the Scottish Cup, were put in storage. In their place came, first, the Regional League, succeeded by the Southern League. Then came the Southern League Cup, a trophy presented by the Scottish F.A., who recalled it when war ended to make it the Victory Cup.

During five of the war years, a Summer Cup was competed for, but Rangers took part in only the first three competitions.

In the years preparatory to the beginning of hostilities, Rangers had been laying the foundations of a reconstructed team, and though impediments, natural to the prevailing circumstances, had to be overcome, there was cause for satisfaction that we, and the game as a whole, stood the test so well.

While there is no necessity to dilate upon our achievements during these war years, it would seem that a brief recording should be given. Rangers' winnings were :—

1939-40—Emergency War Cup, Glasgow Cup, Charity Cup, Regional League.

1940-41—Southern League Cup, Southern League Championship, Glasgow Charity Cup, Scottish Second Eleven Cup.

RANGERS' EVENTFUL YEARS

1941-42—Southern League Cup, Southern League Championship, North-Eastern League (First Series), Glasgow Cup, Glasgow Charity Cup, Summer Cup.

1942-43—Southern League Cup, Southern League Championship, Glasgow Cup.

1943-44—Southern League Championship, Glasgow Cup, Glasgow Charity Cup, Mitchell Cup, North-Eastern Supplementary Cup.

1944-45—Southern League Cup, Southern League Championship, Glasgow Cup, Glasgow Charity Cup.

1945-46—Southern League Championship, Glasgow Charity Cup, Victory Cup.

With the Final of the Victory Cup, at Hampden, the close of hostilities was signalised. Our progress to the Final was by way of Stenhousemuir, whom Rangers defeated home and away by 4–1 in each game ; Airdrieonians (A) 4–0 ; Falkirk (A) 1–1, (H) 2–0 ; Celtic (Hampden) 0–0 and 2–0 ; Final (Hampden), Rangers 3, Hibernian 1.

Teams in the Final were :—

> **Rangers.**—Brown ; Cox and Shaw ; Watkins, Young and Symon ; Waddell, Gillick, Thornton, Duncanson and Caskie.

> **Hibernian.**—Kerr ; Govan and Shaw ; Howie, Aird and Finnigan ; Smith, Peat, Milne, Aitkenhead and Nutley.

Duncanson scored two of Rangers' goals and Gillick one. Aitkenhead scored for Hibernian.

In this Victory Cup competition, played in May and June of 1946, Jimmy Duncanson and Billy Arnison were Rangers' principal marksmen, each with four goals. Duncanson, throughout his stay at Ibrox, could nip in with a goal when it was most required, and his overall record reflects his value to the team.

ONE MORE TRIPLE CROWN.

When the Scottish Cup was won three seasons in succession—1947-48, 1948-49, 1949-50—these eleven players took part in all three Cup competitions.

Back Row (left to right)—W. Waddell, Ian McColl, Geo. Young, Robt. Brown, W. Woodburn, S. Cox.
Sitting—W. Williamson, W. Thornton, J. Shaw, J. Duncanson, E. Rutherford.

[See page 50.

In this cabinet, which stands in the Board Room, there has resided, at various times, every major trophy, the reward of Rangers' victories. The photograph shows some of the souvenirs gifted to the club by Continental clubs.

JAMES DUNCANSON.

	Matches.	Goals.		Matches.	Goals.
1939-40, -	15	5	1945-46, -	5	4
1940-41, -	10	2	1946-47, -	37	23
1941-42, -	5	3	1947-48, -	50	19
1942-43, -	43	24	1948-49, -	40	14
1943-44, -	39	25	1949-50, -	23	5
1944-45, -	32	18			
Matches, 299.			**Goals, 142.**		

Many representative games, especially between Scotland and England, were played on behalf of various funds, but they were unofficial and no caps were awarded.

During part of the war period we were pleased to have as a guest player, Willie McIntosh, a Glasgow laddie, who was on the playing staff of St. Johnstone, who had suspended operations.

Willie, as centre forward, played 57 games for us and scored 48 goals. He would have been glad to remain at Ibrox, and certainly we should have been glad to keep him, but that did not accord with St. Johnstone's desire, and Willie was transferred to Third Lanark. From Cathkin he migrated to Blackpool, by whom, we are delighted to know, he became highly esteemed.

Two years before the outbreak of war, Willie Woodburn had signed, and now he is second long-service man, by only seven months, to Willie Thornton. Edinburgh born, Willie Woodburn set out on what was to be a notable career, as a right half with Ashton Juveniles. Against England, at Leeds, in 1937, he captained Scotland's Juveniles and, later, played seven games for Queen's Park Strollers.

Although now an established centre half, he has taken a turn at right back and right half for Rangers and, in an emergency, grappled bravely with the intricacies of centre forward against Motherwell some five seasons ago.

Representative honours :—Against England 4, Wales 3, Ireland 3, English League 3, Irish League 2, League of Ireland 1 ; in addition to which he had played for Scotland against France, Austria, Portugal, Denmark and Belgium.

His medals include three Scottish Cup and five Scottish League championship, but he hasn't the time to count the others. His games for Rangers (see next page).

33

C

WILLIE WOODBURN.

	Scottish League	Scottish League Cup	Glasgow Cup	Charity Cup	Southern League	Victory Cup	Scottish Cup	Regional League	Southern League Cup	Summer Cup
1938-39,	13	—	—	2	—	—	—	—	—	—
1939-40,	4	—	4	2	—	—	—	29	7	—
1940-41,	—	—	3	2	29	—	—	—	9	5
1941-42,	—	—	—	—	11	—	—	—	—	—
1942-43,	—	—	1	—	1	—	—	—	—	—
1943-44,	—	—	—	—	1	—	—	—	—	—
1944-45,	—	—	1	3	4	—	—	—	4	—
1945-46,	—	—	—	2	20	1	—	—	—	—
1946-47,	18	6	—	—	—	—	—	—	—	—
1947-48,	23	8	4	2	—	—	6	—	—	—
1948-49,	30	7	2	1	—	—	5	—	—	—
1949-50,	29	9	3	2	—	—	8	—	—	—
1950-51,	28	5	2	3	—	—	2	—	—	—

Matches, 361.

Most readers of this Rangers' story will remember our match with the Dynamos, from Russia, in November, 1945 and, certainly, the 90,000, all ticket, who witnessed it will not soon forget it. From Rangers' point of view, the event possessed certain features which could not be described as the acme of friendliness.

Having played three games in England without suffering a reverse, and having been highly praised for their all-round cleverness, the Russians were bent upon making certain that there would be the least possible risk of defeat at the Stadium. A day or two before the match was due, their representatives called on Manager Struth. They wished to know what the Rangers' team was to be, took exception to George Young, who had been off injured, and who, they suspected, was not eligible, and they also objected to Jimmy Caskie, because they regarded him as an Everton player.

Rangers' eleven who took the field were Dawson; David Gray and Shaw; Watkins, Young and Symon; Waddell, Gillick, Smith, Williamson and Johnstone. An agreement was made about substitutes, but it was so freely interpreted by the visitors that at one period in the second half, it was discovered that they had twelve players on the field.

Rangers were two goals down, the first in the third minute, direct from a free kick, before they had time to measure up the opposition, and when they began to fight back, they found that the Dynamo defence did not intend to be of kid-glove variety. Pushing and elbow work, body-checks and so forth, they apparently regarded as good technique. For an infringement by their defence, a penalty was given against them, but Willie Waddell shot straight at the Dynamo custodian.

Then, to show that these Dynamo forwards could produce quality football, a quick, passing swoop, in which the whole line participated, ended with a second goal. What, I think, surprised the Russians more than anything —they admitted to a few surprises before they departed— was the way their opponents came back. The visitors seemed not to like it, and showed the first signs of real anxiety.

Jimmy Smith gave Rangers a goal nearing half-time and, after that, it was almost all Rangers' attack, with Dawson virtually a spectator in the second half. In desperation, the Dynamos called on a substitute centre forward ; later, Jimmy Smith went off and Jimmy Duncanson went on.

In the height of Rangers' pressure, Billy Williamson was clashed, and George Young equalised from the spot.

At the finish, the Dynamo doctor said, " Rangers are the fittest athletes we have ever played against." Their trainer said, " Rangers are easily the best footballers we have played against in Britain. We have no complaint."

Now, the Dynamos were a wonderfully organised force, but here they were lucky to avoid defeat, largely because the Rangers players were capable of weighing-up their strongest points and of countering them accordingly. A lesson is there for whoever cares to take it. As Jimmy Gordon, former Rangers and Scotland half-back, puts it : " No use in making plans *before* the game begins. When play starts, have an eye for the danger spots in the opposition, and your plans will, or should, fall naturally into place."

Season 1941-42 had seen us make a clean sweep, for we won the Southern League Championship, the League Cup, the Glasgow Cup, the Charity Cup and the Summer Cup, besides defeating a powerful R.A.F. eleven at Ibrox, in one of the most keenly contested games, which onlookers voted a genuine football treat.

But these successes were dimmed by the tragic death of Director R. G. Campbell who, previous to his election to the Board, had given yeoman service as a player, whether at back, centre half or centre forward.

To succeed " R. G.," as he was popularly called, there came, virtually from the dressing room to a seat on the Board, George Brown, who had worn the colours since 1929, had won four Scottish Cup medals, and captained Scotland against England as items in a considerable list of honours.

George was what might be described as a product of the famous so-called Intermediate dispute, which, having lasted some four years, had allowed the Junior players involved time to mature their talents before being free to join the senior ranks. Sequel in George Brown's case, as in some others, was that soon he was being senior capped against England, Wales and Ireland and, in fact, finished with nineteen such honours, S.F.A. and League.

Although his favourite position was left half, his manner of using the ball rendered him equally effective in the forward line, and in more than one representative match he figured at inside right. His career as a Ranger is epitomised thus :—

GEORGE BROWN.

	League.	Scottish Cup.	Glasgow Cup.	Charity Cup.	Goals.
1929-30, -	17	5	—	3	—
1930-31, -	29	—	2	3	3
1931-32, -	32	7	4	2	1
1932-33, -	38	4	3	3	—
1933-34, -	35	6	3	2	—
1934-35, -	36	7	2	2	1
1935-36, -	28	6	2	2	2
1936-37, -	35	1	3	1	1
1937-38, -	32	4	3	2	—
1938-39, -	19	2	2	—	2

Matches, 397.

During the first two years of the war he played in 20 games for Rangers.

1946—1947

Neck-and Neck with Hibs—League and Cup Won—
Two Stalwarts Depart—Two Come in.

SO the war was ended. Any fears that the game would take a long time to recover its former hold on the people were soon dispelled. A great resurgence of enthusiasm took place everywhere.

Competition had never been keener, examples of which were the 192 minutes taken by Aberdeen and Dundee to decide their fourth-round Scottish Cup tie, and the 142 minutes required by Hibernian and Motherwell to dispose of their semi-final tie.

In these post-war years it will have been observed how intense has been the rivalry between Hibernian and ourselves in quest of the major prizes. So it was in this season of 1946-47.

It was neck-and-neck with us for the League championship which Rangers won by a mere margin of two points over Hibs. who gave us our first defeat in the League and, later, evicted us from the Scottish Cup in the third round.

Our turn came in the Semi-final of the League Cup, at Hampden and, having beaten that formidable Hibernian combine, we went into the Final to win the Cup with a clear-cut victory against Aberdeen.

Teams who contested that League Cup Final are interesting because, a fortnight later, Aberdeen, with the same eleven, except that Willie Cooper had the bad luck to have to stand down injured, defeated Hibernian in the Scottish Cup Final, and so won the trophy for the first time.

League Cup Final teams :—

> **Rangers.**—Brown ; Young and Shaw ; McColl, Woodburn and Rae ; Rutherford, Gillick, Williamson, Thornton and Duncanson.

> **Aberdeen.**—Johnstone ; Cooper and McKenna ; McLaughlin, Dunlop and Taylor ; Harris, Hamilton, Williams, Baird and McCall

This was the first Final of the Scottish League Cup, a gift from Mr. John McMahon, then League President, and so Rangers became the first club to have their name inscribed on it. Former Southern League Cup, last winners of which had been Aberdeen, had been transmuted into the Victory Cup and, as before related here, Rangers won it to make it their own property.

So, with the League Championship and League Cup added to the Charity Cup, it had been a campaign leaving not much for tears although, at the end of it, we had to regret the departure of Dougie Gray and Jimmy Smith, our two long-service men, who had been pillars of strength over many years.

Dougie was in six Rangers' teams which won the Scottish Cup. He was one of the noble band who brought the Cup to Ibrox three years in succession, an achievement which, though not dreamed of at the time, was to be repeated in the near future by a new company of Rangers' crusaders. Eleven League championship medals were among Dougie's bounteous collection of awards.

As a true-blue sportsman, Dougie Gray could hold his head high. There never was a better. As a junior, he signed in 1925 and was 22 seasons a Ranger.

Jimmy Smith had played twelve games for East Stirlingshire and scored 16 goals when Ibrox called him. Once he had left the boyhood stage behind and become the regular leader of Rangers' attack, he proved one of the most prolific goal-scorers in the country.

An analysis of his scoring feats would find him with over 300 goals in League and Cup matches for Rangers, which takes no account of the goals credited to him on tours and against English teams.

On the lighter side, he earned a kind of fame as the only player who ever charged hefty Joe Kennaway into the net when the Celtic goalkeeper had the ball in his grasp.

RANGERS' EVENTFUL YEARS

1946 - 47.
League Champions.

Scottish Cup.		Glasgow Cup.		Charity Cup.	
Clyde (H),	2–1	Clyde (A),	2–2	Partick Thistle	
A Bye.		Clyde (H),	2–4	(H),	4–0
Hibernian (H),	0–0			Celtic (H),	1–0
Hibernian (A),	0–2				

League Cup.—St. Mirren (H), 4–0 ; (A), 4–0. Queen's Park (H), 1–0 , (A), 4–2. Morton (H), 2–0 , (A), 2–0. Quarter Final—Dundee United (H), 2–1 ; (A), 1–1. Semi-Final—Hibernian (Hampden), 3–1. Final—Aberdeen (Hampden), 4–0

v. England.	v. Wales.	v. Ireland.	v English League.	v Irish League.
G. Young.	W. Waddell	R. Brown.	G Young.	J. Shaw.
J Shaw	W. Thornton	G. Young.	W Woodburn	W. Woodburn.
W. Woodburn		W Thornton	W. Waddell.	T. Gillick.
		J. Duncanson.		

Sam Cox and Bobby Brown had each discarded his amateur status to enter the professional ranks with Rangers in May, 1946.

Sam was of Darvel, and his folks lived a few yards from the renowned Alec Smith, who had played in 34 representative games when Rangers' outside left. Alec took a deep interest in Sam's fondness for the game, and was never tired of imparting to the youngster the benefits of his own experience. Sam pays high tribute to Alec for his invaluable help and encouragement.

From Hurlford Juniors to Queen's Park (two-and-a-half seasons), then three games with Third Lanark, next into uniform, and posted to Aberdeen, which resulted in his tieing up with Dundee, as guest, and still as an amateur—that was the Sam Cox progress.

40

He had been playing two seasons with Dundee when Manager Struth, of " Ours," appeared on the Darvel scene, and, in Redneuk, the Smith domicile, Sam put his name to a Rangers' form. Since that eventful day, Sam has gained all the honours. He makes Stanley Matthews, " the greatest ball player of our time "— and he should know something about that. His Rangers' appearances :—

SAM COX.

	Scottish League.	Scottish League Cup.	Glasgow Cup.	Charity Cup.	Victory Cup.	Scottish Cup.	Goals.
1945-46, - - -	—	—	—	3	6	—	—
1946-47, - - -	13	3	2	1	—	—	2
1947-48, - - -	30	8	4	2	—	7	3
1948-49, - - -	29	9	2	1	—	5	3
1949-50, - - -	30	9	3	1	—	8	7
1950-51, - - -	19	6	1	3	—	2	3

Matches, 225.

RANGERS' EVENTFUL YEARS

It happened that Bobby Brown and Sam Cox made their debut in the same match, which was against Airdrieonians in the Victory Cup. As they came in, Jimmy Smith was going out—this was his farewell game for Rangers.

Goalkeepers, by the nature of their position, are less liable to enforced absence than others, yet it is still a remarkable fact that Bobby Brown has missed only one first-eleven competitive match since he joined Rangers ; that was a League Cup game in his first season. His record with Rangers :—

ROBERT BROWN

	Scottish League	Scottish Cup	League Cup	Glasgow Cup	Charity Cup
1946-47, -	30	3	9	2	2
1947-48, -	30	7	8	4	2
1948-49, -	30 ..	5	9	2	1
1949-50, -	30	8	9	3	2
1950-51, -	30	2	6	2	3
	150	25	41	13	10

Total, 239.

Some of us think that Bobby Brown has not had his fair share of national honours, but I do not imagine it is a matter which would worry him. He has not been capped against England, yet it was against England, at Villa Park as a Queen's Park player, in 1945, in a war-time International, that he gave a display which no goalkeeper could have surpassed. Birmingham fans made a hero of him.

1947—1948

The Three Cups Again—Stern Struggles—Morton's Challenge—League Lost—Glasgow Cup Recovered.

BACK in the glamorous days of the 1890's, when Rangers first brought the Three Cups—Scottish, Glasgow and Charity—to Ibrox, the performance was hailed with a proper feeling of elation.

No one could foresee that in the season of 1947-48 the feat would be accomplished for a fifth time. Nor could we visualise the winning of the Scottish Cup in 1947-48 which was to become the first of three such successive triumphs, an achievement already standing to Rangers' credit, as has been told in previous chapters.

Most remarkable feature of our Scottish Cup ties was that the first against Stranraer on their ground and the Final against Morton, who were then fighting to escape relegation, provided two of our sternest struggles, although the Semi-final tie with Hibernian, at Hampden, was touch-and-go, with only a Thornton goal dividing us at the finish.

As indicative of the tremendous " pull " of a Hibernian-Rangers Cup tie, following the impressive renaissance of the Hibs, the attendance at Hampden was 143,570, still an easy record for a Scottish Cup tie other than a Final.

There is no doubt that the peculiarities of the Stranraer pitch were partly responsible for the Rangers' players being unable to find an effective game, and for creating the possibility of a result that would have been sensational. Here again, a Thornton goal made things right, and we went through to the Final without ourselves having surrendered a goal in the ties.

On their way to the Final, Morton had disposed of Ayr United (H), Falkirk (H), Queen's Park (H), Airdrieonians (A), and Celtic (Ibrox), after extra time. The victory against Celtic had been a signal of danger for Rangers, and it was confirmed by events.

43

RANGERS' EVENTFUL YEARS

It took two games, each with extra time, for the destination of the Cup to be decided. In the first game the line-up was :—

Rangers. — Brown ; Young and Shaw ; McColl, Woodburn and Cox ; Rutherford, Gillick, Thornton, Findlay and Duncanson.

Morton. — Cowan ; Mitchell and Whigham, Campbell, Miller and Whyte ; Hepburn, Murphy, Cupples, Orr and Liddell.

It was a desperately hard, punishing contest right to the last minute of extra time, but neither side could force a winning goal after Whyte had scored for Morton and Gillick for Rangers.

For the replay, Morton let the same eleven try again, but Rangers' forward line became Rutherford, Thornton, Williamson, Duncanson and Gillick.

Another straining tussle ensued. With not a goal on the register after 90 minutes, the tiring rivals went into the extra half-hour once more. The minutes sped by with a hard-fighting Morton defence standing bravely up to a persistent Rangers' attack.

Darkness was coming down and prospects of a decision were fading fast when, less than five minutes to go, there came the long-delayed and vital goal.

Rutherford away over on the left, far from his beat, pushed the ball low towards goal, and Williamson, playing his first and only game in the ties, threw himself down at it in a forlorn attempt to get his head to contact. He succeeded, and before Cowan could make any effective counter move, the ball was in the net and the Cup was won.

Over the two games, the total attendance was 265,199. And Morton fought themselves clear of relegation.

Of the eleven who took part in the Final for Rangers, only Torry Gillick had previously won a Scottish Cup medal. He was our outside-left in the 1934-35 Final when we defeated Hamilton Academicals.

For League honours it was the previous season's story retold, but with the ending reversed. Hibernian won the championship two points better than Rangers.

Defeat from Falkirk in the Semi-Final of the League Cup was a disappointment, but the fact is Rangers did not play well enough to deserve to win.

1947 - 48.

Scottish Cup.		Glasgow Cup.		Charity Cup.	
Stranraer (A),	1–0	Partick Thistle		Partick Thistle	
Leith Athletic		(H),	1–0	(H),	3–0
(H),	4–0	Queen's Park		Celtic	
Partick Thistle		(A),	2–2	(Hampden), 2–0	
(H),	3–0	Queen's Park			
East Fife (H),	1–0	(H),	*3–1		
Hibernian		Third Lanark			
(Hampden), 1–0		(Hampden),	4–1		
*Morton		* After extra time.			
(Hampden), 1–1					
*Morton					
(Hampden), 1–0					
* After extra time.					

League Cup.—Celtic (H), 2–0 , (A), 0–2. Dundee (H), 3–0 ; (A), 1–2. Third Lanark (H), 3–0 ; (A), 3–1. Quarter Final—Stenhousemuir (H), 2–0. Semi-Final—Falkirk (Hampden), 0–1.

v. England.	*v.* Wales.	*v.* Ireland.	*v* English League.	*v.* Irish League.
G. Young	W. Woodburn	G. Young.	G. Young.	G Young.
W. Thornton.		J. Shaw	S. Cox.	S. Cox
		W. Woodburn.	T. Gillick.	T. Gillick.
		W. Thornton		J. Duncanson.

George Young also played against Belgium, Switzerland and France. Sam Cox played against France. Willie Waddell was chosen against England and Eddie Rutherford against Irish League, but both withdrew injured. Rutherford played against France. Willie Woodburn, the lone Ranger, was captain against Wales.

1948—1949

IN their long and eventful career, Rangers have been joint principals in some tense situations, few of which have exceeded in gravity that which existed on the 30th of April, 1949.

We had won the Scottish Cup for the second season in succession, the League Cup reposed once more in the Ibrox cabinet where everything worth winning has found a niche at one time or other.

On that 30th of April the League championship was at stake. By bringing it to Ibrox, Rangers could achieve something no team had yet accomplished—Scottish Cup, League Cup and Championship in one season.

Circumstances seemed unfavourable. Dundee, with Falkirk to meet at Brockville, in their concluding match, were leading us by a point. Rangers, on the same afternoon, were due to engage Albion Rovers at Cliftonhill.

The Taysiders had only to win at Brockville and the championship was theirs, irrespective of what might happen to Rangers at Coatbridge. Dundee had defeated Falkirk at Dens Park and, prior to 30th April, they had lost only one of eight League games. Falkirk had been defeated in their previous four League matches.

Falkirk had gone out of the Scottish Cup in the first round. Dundee had played through to the semi-final. But it was here that the strain imposed on the Taysiders in their laudable ambition to capture one, or both, of the prizes began to take toll. Rangers, in years past, had come to know all about that angle to ambition.

In the crucial test at Brockville, the Dundee players showed facial signs of nervous tension, which became reflected in the efforts of their forwards to translate outfield superiority into goals.

And while Falkirk were taking full advantage, Rangers were making no mistake at Cliftonhill. Their victory and Dundee's defeat sent another championship to Ibrox, to

46

keep the Scottish Cup and the League Cup company, and here are the players who contributed to this unprecedented performance, with their appearances in the three competitions :—

Name.	League.	Scottish. Cup.	League Cup.	Total.
R. Brown, - - -	30	5	9	44
G. Young, - -	28	5	9	42
J. Shaw, - - -	27	5	9	41
I. McColl, - - -	30	5	6	41
W. Woodburn, -	30	5	7	42
W. Waddell, - -	20	5	8	33
S. Cox, - - -	29	5	9	43
W. Paton, - - -	19	4	1	24
W. Thornton, - -	29	5	9	43
W. Findlay, - -	12	—	4	16
T. Gillick, - -	8	—	4	12
J. Duncanson, -	24	5	8	37
E. Rutherford, -	27	5	3	35
W. Williamson, -	6	1	4	11
D. Marshall, - -	3	—	3	6
J. Caskie, - -	1	—	1	2
W. Rae, - - -	1	—	3	4
W. Walmsley, - -	1	—	—	1
J. Lindsay, - -	4	—	2	6
J Frame, - -	1	—	—	1
	330	55	99	484

Until Rangers reached the Final of the Scottish **Cup** the going had been fairly smooth, the only goal lost **being** scored by Elgin City's outside left, Logie, in the first round at Ibrox—a joy day for Logie who, no doubt, still dreams of that goal.

Clyde, who finished third from the bottom of the League that season, gave a good account of themselves in the Final, but two penalties which they conceded, turned the tide against them when George Young converted both.

The line-up was :—

Rangers.—Brown ; Young and Shaw ; McColl, Woodburn and Cox ; Waddell, Duncanson, Thornton, Williamson and Rutherford.

Clyde.—Gullan ; Gibson and Mennie ; Campbell, Milligan and Long ; Davies, Wright, Linwood, Galletly and Bootland.

Billy Williamson, playing his first and only Scottish Cup tie, as also in the previous season's Final, was a scorer, but this time his goal did not require to be decisive.

Play till the whistle is a good old axiom, and its merit was never better exemplified than by our experience in the League Cup. In our section we did not win one of our first three games. There seemed scarcely a hope of recovery. . Celtic had beaten Clyde, Hibernian and ourselves. Question of who should qualify for the Quarter Finals seemed a matter entirely out of our hands.

Then came transformation. With successive victories over Clyde, Hibernian and Celtic, we came bang into the running. Then Clyde, to the surprise of the populace, defeated Celtic at Parkhead, Hibernian followed suit, at Easter Road, tipped the balance in our favour, and we were into the Quarter Finals.

We Value These Trophies

Here is the story of two trophies won by Rangers in the early period of the war Players who took part in the two matches in which these trophies were at stake, affirm that in none of thir contests, before or since, did they experience a keener sense of rivalry or a greater thrill in winning.

Of all the trophies in permanent possession of the Rangers Club, none is more valued than the silver casket won, in 1941, by virtue of a victory over Preston North End, at the Stadium.

The match was on behalf of the Glasgow War Fund. Sir Patrick Dollan, then Lord Provost, received the ready consent of Preston North End to meet Rangers. He offered to present a trophy which would become the property of the winning club.

Designs were invited, and the Lord Provost chose that which formed a replica of the casket in which the heart of King Robert the Bruce was brought back from Spain.

The match aroused the keenest interest, for it was realised that it was to be a real contest. So, on the evening of 1st September, 1941, there was an attendance of 35,000 at the Stadium. £2,350 was drawn.

Both clubs fielded their strongest possible teams which lined up thus :—

> *Rangers.*—Dawson ; Gray and Shaw ; Little, Woodburn and Symon ; McIntosh, Gillick, Smith, Venters and Beattie.

> *Preston North End.*—Fairbrother ; A. Beattie and Scott ; Shankly, Smith and Manley ; Finney, McLaren, Dougal, R. Beattie and O'Donnell.

From first to last it was a fast, exciting tussle, and though Rangers won, our visitors earned the highest praise for their share in making it a match worthy of the purpose for which it had been organised.

When the final whistle sounded, thousands of enthusiastic spectators rushed on to the field to cheer, again and again, the players of the two teams who lined up to receive War Savings Certificates.

On 23rd April, 1941, on the invitation of Sir Archibald Sinclair, then Minister of Air, Rangers played a match against a team representing the R.A.F., the proceeds to be divided between the Clydeside Raid Distress Fund and the Air Force Benevolent Fund.

Sir Archibald presented this trophy to be held for all time by the winners. Rangers won, and the trophy has an honoured place alongside others which, from time to time, have been either won by or gifted to the club.

At that time the R.A.F. was capable of putting a strong eleven on the field. We realised that we should require to put forth our best effort. Alec Venters scored the only goal of the first half, but our prospects did not seem encouraging when, near the interval, Bobby Bolt was injured. He went to outside right, Willie Waddell going inside, and Willie Thornton to right-half.

Rangers played the first minute and a half after the interval without Bobby Bolt and Jimmy Smith, but they ran on to the field just in time to see Charlie Johnstone score our second goal. But there was plenty of fight in the airmen yet. Two minutes later, Kirchen beat Jerry Dawson with a terrific drive from an angle, and in the next minute Jerry made a brilliant save from Gibbons.

Then came a spectacular goal, Rangers' third, by Jimmy Smith. Still, the airmen would not admit defeat. Kirchen scored again with the cheers for our third goal still filling the arena. It was a thrilling finish, with the airmen going all out for an equalising goal, but Rangers' defence held out.

The Sinclair Trophy was won by 3 goals to 2. Congratulations well earned by losers as well as winners.

There we had a tough job beating St. Mirren at Ibrox, by a Thornton goal, and having beaten Dundee in the Semi-Final, we went to Hampden for the Final with Raith Rovers :—

Rangers.—Brown ; Young and Shaw ; McColl, Woodburn and Cox ; Gillick, Paton, Thornton, Duncanson and Rutherford.

Raith Rovers.—Westland ; McLure and McNaught ; Young, Colville and Leigh ; Maule, Collins, Penman, Brady and Joyner.

Rovers later became B Division champions, and we knew them to be a sound combine, fore and aft. They gave us one of our hardest contests of the entire season, and we were pleased to survive with a goal each by Torry Gillick and Willie Paton.

So a notable season had ended, leaving something good to come in 1949–50.

1948 - 49.
League Champions.

Scottish Cup.		Glasgow Cup.		Charity Cup.	
Elgin City (H),	6–1	Clyde (A),	2–1	Partick Thistle	
Motherwell (A),	3–0	Third Lanark		(H),	0–1
A Bye.		(A),	1–4		
Partick Thistle (H),	4–0				
East Fife					
(Hampden),	3–0				
Clyde (Hampden),	4–1				

League Cup.—Celtic (H), 2–1 ; (A), 1–3. Clyde (H), 1–1 ; (A), 3–1. Hibernian (H), 1–0 ; (A), 0–0. Quarter Final—St. Mirren (H), 1–0. Semi-Final—Dundee (Hampden), 4–1. Final—Raith Rovers (Hampden), 2–0.

v. England.	*v.* Wales.	*v.* Ireland.	*v.* English League.	*v.* Irish League.
G. Young.	G. Young.	R. Brown	R. Brown.	G. Young.
S. Cox.	W. Waddell.	G. Young	G. Young.	S. Cox.
W. Woodburn.		W. Waddell.	W. Thornton.	W. Waddell.
W. Waddell.				

Thornton was travelling reserve against England, Cox against Ireland. Young, Cox, Woodburn, Waddell and Thornton played against France.

49

1949—1950

I N the testing trials of this adventurous game of ours,
nothing is predictable, but, whatever may come to
Rangers in future years, this season of 1949–50
should be remembered as a bright and shining phase in a
career which has not been without others of its kind.

We became champions of the Scottish League for
the twenty-seventh time (including once jointly with
Dumbarton). We won the Scottish Cup for the third
successive season, and though the all-in League performance
no doubt took a higher place in actual merit, sentimentally
our Cup triumph was, for various reasons, accepted as the
crowning victory.

As those who have followed this narrative from the
beginning are aware, we had before brought the Cup to
Ibrox in three successive seasons, a fact which rendered
this new achievement the more noteworthy.

When the draw indicated a visit to Fir Park in the first
round, we saw danger, for, a week or two before the ballot
took place, we had suffered, at Fir Park, one of our only
two defeats in the League. But our traditional good
fortune in the Cup at Fir Park held, and we got through
by a two-goal margin.

We had still a long way to go, however. A clever,
resolute Raith Rovers gave us three desperately hard
games—the one at Stark's Park, with extra time thrown
in—before we were free to tackle Queen of the South in
the semi-final.

It was a case of the struggle to be continued. **At** Hampden, the men from Palmerston fought us foot-to-foot, J. Brown capping a goal by our Eddie Rutherford. Back again to Hampden, we cleared the hurdle, but a 3–0 score in our favour did scant justice to our opponents.

So we were face-to-face in the Final with East Fife who had beaten us in the League Cup Semi-Final, and this was the line-up :—

> **Rangers.**—Brown ; Young and Shaw ; McColl, Woodburn and Cox ; Rutherford, Findlay, Thornton, Duncanson and Rae.

> **East Fife.**—Easson ; Laird and Stewart ; Philp, Findlay and Aitken ; Black, Fleming, Morris, Brown and Duncan.

In commenting on the result, our former left-half, Scott Symon, by then manager of East Fife, summed it up when he said, " I never saw Rangers play better."

It was one of our very good days, and we had quite a few in our march to the championship.

Thornton, a dashing leader of the attack in the Final, appropriately scored two of Rangers' goals, and Findlay the other one.

Nineteen players shared in the three-seasons' Cup triumph, but only Bobby Brown, George Young, Sam Cox and Ian McColl played in every game over the three seasons. Jock Shaw and Willie Woodburn each missed one game, Willie Thornton missed two, and Eddie Rutherford four.

Here are the appearances of the players :—

THE   THREE-CUP   VICTORS.

	1947-48.	1948-49.	1949-50.	Total.
R Brown, -	7	5	8	20
G. Young, -	7	5	8	20
J. Shaw. -	7	5	7	19
S. Cox, - -	7	5	8	20
I. McColl, -	7	5	8	20
W. Woodburn,	6	5	8	19
W. Rae, -	1	—	3	4
W. Waddell, -	3	5	3	11
T. Gillick, -	7	—	—	7
W. Williamson,	1	1	7	9
W. Thornton,	7	5	6	18
J. Duncanson,	7	5	2	14
J Caskie, -	3	—	—	3
J. Rutherford,	6	5	5	16
W. Findlay,	1	—	7	8
W. Paton, -	—	4	3	7
J. Johnson, -	—	—	2	2
W. McCulloch,	—	—	2	2
J. Lindsay, -	—	—	1	1
	77	55	88	220

As if still further to emphasise the growing affinity between Hibernian and Rangers, they made one more running fight for League honours.   When the last Saturday of April arrived, they were listed to meet in their postponed Ibrox fixture, which could be vital to both.   This was the position :

VICTORS OF 1946—1947.

Back Row (Left to Right)—Director-Manager Struth, Sam Cox, George Young, Ian McColl, Robert Brown, Willie Woodburn, Charles Watkins, William Rae, Robert McDonald (Trainer).

Front Row—James Caskie (Inset), William Waddell, Torry Gillick, John Shaw, William Williamson, William Thornton, James Duncanson, Eddy Rutherford (Inset).

(The Victory Cup was competed for in May and June, 1946).

A FEAT UNEQUALLED.

[*Photo by* T. & R. ANNAN.

In Season 1048-49 an unprecedented feat was accomplished by Rangers when they won the Scottish Cup, League Championship Cup and League Cup (Section and Final). Number of games played by the respective players are appended to names :—

BACK ROW (*left to right*).—*Director-Manager* Struth; W. Waddell (41); I. McColl (33); G. Young (42); R. Brown (44); W. Woodburn (42); W. Findlay (16); W. Rae (4); J. Duncanson (37); J. Smith (*Trainer*).

SITTING.—E. Rutherford (35); T. Gillick (12); W. Thornton (48); J. Shaw (41); W. Williamson (11); S. Cox (43); J. Caskie (2).

See page 46

Hibs had beaten Rangers at Easter Road by a Turnbull goal. They themselves had twice lost to Hearts and, much to the astonishment of everybody, had surrendered both points at Easter Road to Third Lanark, whom they had beaten at Cathkin. These were Hibs' only three reverses.

Rangers' only defeat, apart from the one at Easter Road, had been inflicted by Motherwell at Fir Park.

When the rivals lined up at Ibrox on that April Saturday, with over 100,000 spectators all on edge—you may be sure—it was Hibs' last chance. Rangers had still one match to go, which was Third Lanark at Cathkin, two days later.

If Hibs. could beat Rangers, the championship was for Easter Road, since their then aggregate of 50 points could only be equalled by Rangers beating Third Lanark and, even then, Hibs. would be champions on goal average.

But good-bye to " ifs " and " buts." Hibs. could do no more than draw, and when Rangers did likewise at Cathkin, another championship—the third in four seasons—was sealed for Ibrox by a single point. And a telegram of congratulation promptly reached the Stadium from London—from Hibs., no less ; they were on their way to Vienna.

1949 - 50.
League Champions.

Scottish Cup.		Glasgow Cup.		Charity Cup.	
Motherwell (A),	4–2	Celtic (A),	2–1	Partick Thistle	
A Bye.		Clyde		(H),	4–0
Raith Rovers		(Hampden), 2–2		Celtic	
(Hampden),	1–1	Clyde		(Hampden), 2–3	
Raith Rovers (A),	*1–1	(Hampden), *2–1			
Raith Rovers (H),	2–1				
Queen of the South					
(Hampden),	1–1				
Queen of the South					
(Hampden),	3–0				
East Fife					
(Hampden),	3–0				

* Denotes extra time.

53

RANGERS' EVENTFUL YEARS

1949 - 50.

League Cup.—Aberdeen (H), 4–2 ; (A), 1–1. Celtic (H) 2–0 ; (A), 2–3. St. Mirren (H), 5–1 ; (A), 1–1. Quarter Final— Cowdenbeath (H), 2–3 ; (A), *3–1. Semi-Final—East Fife (Hampden), *1–2.   * Extra time.

v. England.	v. Wales.	v. Ireland.	v. English League.	v. Irish League.
G. Young.	G Young.	G. Young.	R. Brown.	G. Young.
S. Cox	S. Cox.	S. Cox.	G. Young.	S. Cox.
I. McColl.	W. Woodburn.	W. Woodburn.	S. Cox.	W. Woodburn.
W. Woodburn		W. Waddell.	W. Woodburn.	W. Waddell.
W. Waddell.				

Young, Cox and Woodburn played against France and Portugal ; Ian McColl against France ; Young and Cox against Switzerland. Young, Cox and Woodburn played against League of Ireland.

Some good people take the view that captaincy doesn't mean a thing, that the team would play just the same if there wasn't any. By contrast, I once heard an International player say of a team-mate, who was also captain, " So long as he is on the field I would never give up, even if we were half-a-dozen goals down."

If the captain is the man he should be, the example he sets can be of priceless value. Here, Rangers are fortunate in having had in John (Jock) Shaw the type of leader who fulfils the essentials—never-say-die, fair to all—opponents and team-mates—quietly proud in victory and no bitterness in defeat.

" Thirteen years at Ibrox, and I wish I had it all to go through again," is how Jock sums it up. He was captain when Rangers won the Scottish Cup in these three successive seasons ; captain, too, when they became League champions in three of the four seasons following the end of the war.

At Wembley, four years ago, he led Scotland's gallants to a praiseworthy draw. Jock rates Stanley Matthews one of the greatest ever, and, after that day at Wembley, Stanley should have formed a favourable opinion of Jock Shaw.

Here is his record of appearances for Rangers, and though he keeps it dark, he has three goals standing to his credit— one of them for Airdrieonians :—

54

JOHN SHAW.

	Scottish League.	Scottish League Cup	Glasgow Cup.	Charity Cup.	Southern League.	Victory Cup.	Scottish Cup.	Regional League.	Southern League Cup.	Summer Cup.
1938-39,	36	—	2	2	—	—	3	—	—	—
1939-40,	4	—	4	2	—	—	—	28	7	—
1940-41,	—	—	3	2	29	—	—	—	9	6
1941-42,	—	—	2	3	29	—	—	—	8	6
1942-43,	—	—	3	1	30	—	—	—	8	6
1943-44,	—	—	2	2	28	—	—	—	7	—
1944-45,	—	—	3	3	29	—	—	—	8	—
1945-46,	—	—	2	2	27	8	—	—	9	—
1946-47,	28	6	2	2	—	—	3	—	—	—
1947-48,	28	8	4	1	—	—	7	—	—	—
1948-49,	27	9	1	1	—	—	5	—	—	—
1949-50,	29	9	2	2	—	—	7	—	—	—
1950-51,	18	6	1	3	—	—	2	—	—	—

Matches, 576.

55

1950—1951

A Change of Fortune—Trophies Lost—League
Runners-up—Our Players Honoured—Dynamo
Episode.

THERE need be no beating about the bush in regard
to 1950-51. No doubt, any of our rivals who came
up behind us in the League would have been satisfied
to finish runners-up, as we did, on goal average over
Dundee. With our performances of past years, however,
our figures on the final League table compared not at all
well. In so many words, the results, not only in the
League, but in League Cup, Glasgow Cup and Charity Cup,
fell below acknowledged Rangers' standard, and that is
not forgetting that we won the Charity Cup.

We had to part with the Scottish Cup, League
championship and Glasgow Cup, a circumstance which
might have hurt more keenly but for the fact that
Rangers' teams have had experiences nearly similar in
years gone by, and have never failed to come back more
virile than before.

In retrospect, it is easy to see where points lost could,
and should, have been gained. Nine defeats in the League
was out of all proportion to Rangers' normal and, while
not withholding a particle of credit due to Hibernian, our
reverse at their hands in the second round of the Scottish
Cup left a sense of self-frustration, which must have been
keenly felt by our loyal supporters among the 105,000
spectators.

For the first time since the League Cup was instituted,
Rangers failed to qualify for the knock-out ties. We had
won the competition in six of its ten years' existence,

first as the Southern League Cup, and then as the new trophy gifted to the Scottish League by Mr. John McMahon, in 1946, when he was League President.

We could not complain at not having had our share of it.

Although this, primarily, is a Rangers story, our interests are interwoven with those of all the clubs whom we meet in competition, and naturally, perhaps, we follow more particularly the fortunes of our rivals who may have adversely influenced our own ambitions. From that standpoint we feel that, without pretence, we can extend to our rivals of Easter Road a word of sympathy on the Scottish Cup and League Cup having again eluded them when prospects of success appeared so bright. It is simply because we ourselves have experienced such disappointments that we can appreciate theirs.

At the same time, it is pleasant to be able to congratulate Hibernian on being League champions for the second time in four seasons. To achieve such a performance calls for consistency of a high order.

As in previous years, many representative honours were accorded our players who contributed to Scotland's victories against England, Wales and Ireland, and to the Scottish League's success against the English League and Irish League.

1950-51.

Scottish Cup.	Glasgow Cup.	Charity Cup.
Queen of the South (H), 2–0	Partick Thistle (H). 2–2	Celtic (Hampden), 2–1
Hibernian (H), 2–3	Partick Thistle (A), 1–1	Third Lanark (Hampden), *1–1
	Thistle won on toss of coin after extra time.	Partick Thistle (Hampden), 2–0
		Rangers won on toss.

RANGERS' EVENTFUL YEARS

League Cup.—Aberdeen (H), 1–2 ; (A), 0–2. Clyde (H), 4–0 , (A), 5–1. Morton (H), 6–1 ; (A), 2–1.

v. England.	v. Wales.	v. Ireland.	v. English League.	v. Irish League.
G. Young	G. Young	G. Young.	R. Brown.	R. Brown
S. Cox.	I. McColl.	I. McColl.	G. Young.	G. Young
W. Woodburn.	W. Woodburn.	W. Woodburn.	W. Woodburn.	S. Cox.
W. Waddell.				E. Rutherford.

Cox was chosen against Wales, but withdrew injured. Brown, Young and Cox played against the League of Ireland (Eire).

George Young had the distinction of playing in every representative match, as captain, including those against France, Belgium and Austria. In all these games he was right back, although he was signed as a left back, and playing mostly at centre half before taking over the right back position.

It was as pivot that he played for Rangers against the Dynamo eleven—twelve for a short period—at Ibrox in November, 1945. When the Russians came to Ibrox, many who had seen them in England thought them invincible, but Rangers had them in distress all through the second half and, with their mechanism thrown out of gear, they were, no doubt, pleased to draw. But no one could deny the specialised skill of those Dynamos, so long as they were able to command the initiative. Rangers took it from them, and George Young had a big share in that by dominating their inside forwards. His appearances for Rangers in competitive games are here shown:—

58

GEORGE YOUNG.

	Scottish League.	Scottish League Cup.	Glasgow Cup.	Charity Cup.	Scottish Cup.	Summer Cup.	Victory Cup.
1941-42, -	25	8	—	2	—	6	—
1942-43, -	29	8	2	1	—	6	—
1943-44, -	29	8	2	2	—	—	—
1944-45, -	29	8	3	3	—	—	—
1945-46, -	12	9	2	1	—	—	7
1946-47, -	28	5	2	1	3	—	—
1947-48, -	15	4	3	2	7	—	—
1948-49, -	28	9	2	—	5	—	—
1949-50, -	33	9	3	2	8	—	—
1950-51, -	30	5	2	3	2	—	—

Matches, 413.

Now, as elected club captain, he has the opportunity to turn to advantage his experience in leadership of Scotland's representative teams. Four seasons in succession as Scotland's captain against England is an experience without parallel by any player past or present.

59

BIRTH AND AFTER.

SEVENTY-EIGHT years ago, a band of youths from the Gareloch, who had come to the "big city" to woo fame and fortune decided, in a moment of prophetic imagination, to form a football club. Thus, the Glasgow Rangers, or just Rangers, as we prefer it. They took the name Rangers from an English football annual. To-day it is known the world over and, we like to think, respected in some degree.

Changes there have been since those Gareloch enthusiasts first kicked a ball on the open spaces of Glasgow Green, and none, perhaps, more significant than that embodied in the present Ibrox Stadium. It comprises over fifteen acres, with measured accommodation for 136,940 spectators. On the grand stand there are tip-up chairs for 10,294 persons. Greatest attendance to date, 118,567 on the occasion of League match with Celtic, 2nd January, 1939.

The grand stand cost £63,696, the administrative block, £17,993. During the past close season the entire playing pitch was returfed at a cost of £15,000, and received an appropriate inauguration with the annual sports which, thanks to the organising genius of Director-Manager Struth, have, over the years, obtained world-wide fame.

To meet any emergency on match days, the Eastwood Section of St. Andrew's Ambulance Corps, in charge of Commandant W. Macrae, has done voluntary duty on the ground since 1907. We pay them tribute. One, also, to the Govan Burgh Band for their renderings, calculated to soothe the nerves of supporters anxious about what is to happen when the game begins.

OUR PLAYERS FOR SEASON 1951-52.

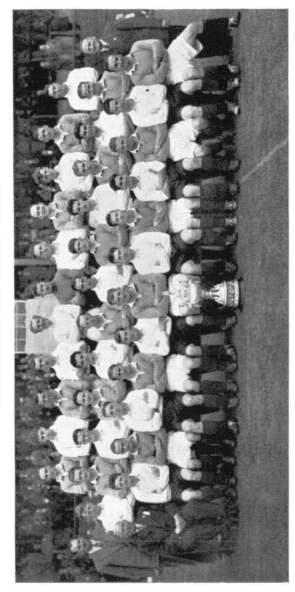

BACK ROW.—I. McColl, W. Boyd, J. Little, A. Elliott, R. Brown, G. Niven, J. Johnson, W. Rae, J. Forbes, E. Rutherford, A. Miller.

MIDDLE ROW.—J. Smith (*Trainer*), L. Blyth, W. Woodburn, A. McPhail, W. Waddell, W. McCulloch, W. Paton, W. Findlay, D. Stanners, R. Dunlop, J. Prentice, J. Pryde, W. Thornton, J. Craven (*Assistant Trainer*).

FRONT ROW.—Mr. Struth (*Director-Manager*), W. Beckett, J. Hubbard, W. Simpson, S. Cox, R. Simpson, G. Young, D. Marshall, J. Woods, G. Scobie, J. Shaw, A. Simpson, W. Williamson.

TRAGEDY ENTERS.

DURING the war period the club sustained a grievous loss by the death of Director R. G. (Bob) Campbell who, first as player and later, for sixteen years on the Board, had earned the highest regard of his team-mates and co-directors.

Bob had no exaggerated notions of his ability as a player, but, for all that, he gave invaluable service as back, the position for which he was signed, in 1906, and as centre-forward. At first he treated his installation at centre as not to be taken too seriously, but he got a lot of goals to which the team owed some of their most prized victories.

To fill the vacancy on the Board, Mr. G. C. P. Brown was invited to join two former Rangers' International players, in James Bowie and Alan Morton, and he is now in his eleventh season as a Director.

Like his two co-directors, George Brown had gained International honours when a Rangers player. As left half, he was in four Rangers' teams that won the Scottish Cup, and he was one of the noted company which first accomplished the feat of taking the trophy to the Stadium in three successive seasons. In season 1933-34, when the Rangers won the Scottish, Glasgow and Charity Cups and the League Championship, George played 46 of the total 50 matches in the four competitions.

Another serious misfortune befel the club by the death of Mr. William Roger Simpson, in 1949. Following the tragic death by drowning, in 1920, of Mr. William Wilton, our first manager-secretary, Mr. Simpson became secretary, and he acted in that capacity until elected to the Board of Directors at the annual meeting in 1947. His co-directors thereupon elected him chairman in succession to Mr. James Bowie, who had occupied that position for eleven seasons. To succeed Mr. Simpson as secretary his son James was unanimously chosen by the directors.

At the annual meeting in 1947, the Board was increased from three to five members by the election of Councillor John F. Wilson and Manager William Struth. Councillor Wilson was made vice-chairman and, on the death of Mr. Simpson, he became chairman, and Mr. Struth, vice-chairman, while the vacancy on the Board was filled by the appointment of Ex-Bailie Gordon Bennett.

TREASURED GIFTS.

IN February, 1948, we had the pleasure of paying a visit to Lisbon in response to an invitation to play the Benfica club. It was a delightful outing, from the moment we boarded the 'plane at Prestwick until we touched down at the same airport two days later. Our hosts treated us to lavish hospitality. Each of our players received the gift of a handsome cigarette case, while Director-Manager Struth accepted, on behalf of the club, a beautiful model of a carvel such as Portuguese adventurers of olden days sailed uncharted seas. It was accompanied by a richly embroidered banner, suitably commemorating our visit.

Rangers reciprocated by presenting to the Benfica club a piece of silver plate appropriately inscribed, and to each of the players a silver propelling pencil, along with a Rangers' club badge.

During the close season of 1950, we had to decline several invitations to go on tours abroad because of conditions affecting our players, which the Scottish F.A. invoked, but, before the new season had got properly under way, we were able to answer a warm invitation from Denmark.

We played three games in Copenhagen, won the first two and lost the third, which, of course, indicated a return match at the Stadium. This was duly carried out, and we won a fine sporting game with the Academiste Boldklub, thus maintaining our record of never having lost at home to a Continental side.

Carl Hansen came with the Danish party as a guest of the Rangers club. He was accorded a warm welcome by Rangers' followers who remembered him as a laddie from Copenhagen, who knew scarcely a word of English, was " fathered " by Director-Manager Struth, and played some very fine football for us at centre forward before injury necessitated his return home. His first thought on reaching Glasgow with the Danish team, was to visit Director-Manager Struth who was then a patient in Victoria Infirmary.

At the dinner which followed the game, our chairman, Mr. John Wilson, accepted, on behalf of the club, a handsome vase of Danish china.

RANGERS' VICTORY YEARS.

RANGERS' VICTORY YEARS.

Scottish Cup.	Glasgow Cup.	Charity Cup.	Scottish League.	Scottish 2nd XI Cup.	Alliance C'pionships
—	—	1878-79	—	—	—
—	—	—	—	1889-90	—
—	—	—	1890-91*	—	—
—	1892-93	—	—	—	—
1893-94	1893-94	—	—	—	—
—	—	—	—	—	1894-95
1896-97	1896-97	1896-97	—	—	—
1897-98	1897-98	—	—	1897-98	—
—	—	—	1898-99	1898-99	1898-99
—	1899-1900	1899-1900	1899-1900	—	—
—	1900-01	—	1900-01	—	—
—	1901-02†	—	1901-02	—	—
1902-03	—	—	—	—	—
—	—	1903-04	—	—	—
—	—	1905-06	—	—	1905-06
—	—	1906-07	—	1906-07	—
—	—	1908-09	—	—	—
—	—	—	—	—	1909-10
—	1910-11	1910-11	1910-11	—	1910-11
—	1911-12	—	1911-12	1911-12	1911-12
—	1912-13	—	1912-13	1912-13	1912-13
—	1913-14	—	—	—	—
—	—	—	—	—	1914-15
—	1917-18	—	1917-18	—	—
—	1918-19	1918-19	—	—	—
—	—	—	1919-20	—	—
—	—	—	1920-21	—	—
—	1921-22	1921-22	—	—	—
—	1922-23	1922-23	1922-23	—	—
—	1923-24	—	1923-24	1923-24	1923-24
—	1924-25	1924-25	1924-25	1924-25	—
—	—	—	—	1925-26	—
—	—	—	1926-27	—	—
1927-28	—	1927-28	1927-28	1927-28	1927-28

RANGERS' VICTORY YEARS

Scottish Cup.	Glasgow Cup.	Charity Cup.	Scottish League.	Scottish 2nd XI Cup	Alliance C'pionships
—	—	1928-29	1928-29	1928-29	1928-29
1929-30	1929-30	1929-30	1929-30	1929-30	1929-30
—	—	1930-31	1930-31	1930-31	1930-31
1931-32	1931-32	1931-32	—	—	1931-32
—	1932-33	1932-33	1932-33	1932-33	—
1933-34	1933-34	1933-34	1933-34	—	—
1934-35	—	—	1934-35	—	1934-35
1935-36	1935-36	—	—	—	—
—	1936-37	—	1936-37	1936-37	—
—	1937-38	—	—	1937-38	—
—	—	1938-39	1938-39	—	1938-39
—	1939-40	1939-40	—	—	—
—	—	1940-41	—	1940-41	—
—	1941-42	1941-42	—	—	—
—	1942-43	—	—	—	—
—	1943-44	1943-44	—	—	—
—	1944-45	1944-45	—	—	—
—	—	1945-46	—	—	—
—	—	1946-47	1946-47	—	—
1947-48	1947-48	1947-48	—	—	—
1948-49	—	—	1948-49	—	—
1949-50	1949-50	—	1949-50	—	—
—	—	1950-51	—	—	—
13	**31**	**29**	**27**	**17**	**16**

* Joint Champions with Dumbarton.

† Celtic scratched.

65

OUR SCOTTISH CUP WINNING TEAMS

1893 - 4.
D. Haddow.
N. Smith.
J. Drummond
R Marshall
A. McCreadie.
D. Mitchell.
J Steel
H McCreadie.
J. Gray
J McPherson.
J Barker

Rangers   3
Celtic   1

1896 - 7.
M Dickie.
N Smith
J. Drummond.
N Gibson
A McCreadie.
D Mitchell.
T Low.
J. McPherson.
J. Miller
T. Hyslop.
A. Smith.

Rangers   5
Dumbarton   1

1897 - 8.
M. Dickie.
N. Smith.
J. Drummond.
N. Gibson.
R. G Neil.
D. Mitchell.
J. Miller.
J. McPherson.
R. C. Hamilton
T Hyslop.
A. Smith.

Rangers   2
Kilmarnock   0

1902 - 3.
M Dickie
A. Fraser.
J. Drummond.
G Henderson.
J. Stark
J T Robertson.
A. Macdonald.
A. Mackie
R C Hamilton.
F. Speedie.
A. Smith.

Rangers   2
Hearts   0

1927 - 8.
T. Hamilton.
D. Gray
R. Hamilton.
J. Buchanan.
D. Meiklejohn.
T. Craig
A. Archibald.
A. Cunningham.
J. Fleming
R McPhail.
A L. Morton.

Rangers   4
Celtic   0

1929 - 30.
T. Hamilton.
D Gray
R Hamilton
R. McDonald.
D. Meiklejohn.
T. Craig
A Archibald.
J. Marshall
J. Fleming.
R. McPhail.
A. L. Morton.

Rangers   2
Partick Th.   1

1931 - 2.
T. Hamilton.
D Gray.
R McAulay.
D. Meiklejohn.
J. Simpson.
G. Brown.
A. Archibald.
J Marshall.
S. English
R McPhail
J. Fleming.

Rangers   3
Kilmarnock   0

1933 - 4.
T. Hamilton
D. Gray
R McDonald.
D. Meiklejohn
J Simpson.
G. Brown
R. Main
J. Marshall.
J. Smith
R McPhail
W. G Nicholson.

Rangers   5
St. Mirren   0

1934 - 5.
J. Dawson.
D. Gray.
R. McDonald.
J. Kennedy.
J. Simpson.
G. Brown.
R. Main.
A. Venters.
J. Smith.
R. McPhail.
T. Gillick.

Rangers   2
Hamilton   1

1935 - 6.
J. Dawson.
D. Gray.
A. Cheyne
D. Meiklejohn.
J. Simpson.
G Brown
J Fiddes.
A. Venters.
J Smith.
R McPhail.
J. Turnbull.

Rangers   1
Th. Lanark   0

1947 - 8.
R. Brown
G. Young
J Shaw
I McColl
W Woodburn.
S Cox
E Rutherford.
W Thornton
W. Williamson.
J. Duncanson
T. Gillick

Rangers   1
Morton   0

1948 - 9.
R. Brown.
G. Young
J. Shaw
I. McColl
W. Woodburn.
S Cox
W. Waddell.
J. Duncanson
W. Thornton.
W Williamson
E. Rutherford.

Rangers   4
Clyde   1

1949 - 50.
R. Brown
G Young
J. Shaw
I. McColl

W. Woodburn
S Cox
E. Rutherford
W. Findlay

W. Thornton
J. Duncanson
W Rae.

Rangers   3   *East Fife*   0

66

RANGERS' SCOTTISH CUP RECORD.

1873-74.
Rangers did not compete.

1874-75.

Round.		Opponents.				Ground
FIRST ROUND.	2 ;	Oxford,	-	-	0	Queen's Park.
SECOND ROUND.	0 ;	Dumbarton,	-	-	0	Glasgow Green.
REPLAY.	0 ;	Dumbarton,	-	-	1	Dumbarton.

1875-76.

FIRST ROUND.	7 ;	1st L.R.V.,	-	-	0	Burnbank.
SECOND ROUND.	0 ;	Third Lanark,		-	2	Cathkin Park.

1876-77.

FIRST ROUND.	4 ;	Queen's Park Juniors,	1	Kinning Park.
SECOND ROUND.	8 ;	Towerhill, - -	0	Springburn.
THIRD ROUND.	A Bye.			
FOURTH ROUND.	3 ;	Mauchline, - -	0	Mauchline.
FIFTH ROUND.	3 ;	Lennox, - -	0	Dumbarton.
SEMI-FINAL.	A Bye.			
FINAL.	0 ;	Vale of Leven, -	0	Hamilton Cres.
REPLAY.	1 ;	Vale of Leven, -	1	Hamilton Cres.
REPLAY.	2 ;	Vale of Leven, -	3	Hampden Park.

1877-78.

FIRST ROUND.	13 ;	Possilpark, - -	0	Kinning Park.
SECOND ROUND.	8 ;	Alexandra Athletic,	0	Kinning Park.
THIRD ROUND.	13 ;	Uddingston, - -	0	Kinning Park.
FOURTH ROUND.	0 ;	Vale of Leven, -	0	Kinning Park.
REPLAY.	0 ;	Vale of Leven, -	5	Alexandria.

RANGERS' EVENTFUL YEARS

1878-79.

Round.		Opponents.				Ground.
FIRST ROUND.	3 ,	Shaftesbury,	-	-	0	Kinning Park.
SECOND ROUND.	6 ;	Whitefield,	-	-	1	Whitefield Park.
THIRD ROUND.	8 ;	Parkgrove,	-	-	2	Kinning Park.
FOURTH ROUND.	3 ;	Alexandra Athletic,		0		Kinning Park.
FIFTH ROUND.	4 ;	Partick	-	-	0	Kinning Park.
SIXTH ROUND.	1 ;	Queen's Park,		-	0	Hampden Park.
SEMI-FINAL.	A Bye.					
FINAL.	1 ;	Vale of Leven,		-	1	Hampden Park.

A protest by Rangers on the ground that they
had scored a second goal was not sustained by
the S.F.A., and they declined to replay. Vale
of Leven were, therefore, awarded the Cup.

1879-80.

FIRST ROUND	0 ;	Queen's Park,		-	0	Kinning Park.
REPLAY.	1 ;	Queen's Park,		-	5	Hampden Park.

1880-81.

FIRST ROUND.	4 ;	Govan,	-	-	1	Kinning Park.
SECOND ROUND.	1 ;	Northern,	-	-	0	Springburn.
THIRD ROUND.	3 ;	Partick Thistle,		-	0	Kinning Park.
FOURTH ROUND.	11 ;	Clyde,	-	-	0	Kinning Park.
FIFTH ROUND.	3 ;	Hurlford,	-	-	0	Hurlford.
SIXTH ROUND.	1 ;	Dumbarton,	-	-	3	Dumbarton.

1881-82.

FIRST ROUND.	2 ;	Third Lanark,		-	1	Kinning Park.
SECOND ROUND.	W.O.	Harmonic. Scratched.				
THIRD ROUND.	3 ;	Alexandra Athletic,		1		Kinning Park.
FOURTH ROUND.	2 ;	Thornliebank,		-	0	Thornliebank.
FIFTH ROUND	6 ;	South Western,		-	4	Kinning Park.

After a protested game, won by Rangers, 2–1.

SIXTH ROUND.	1 ;	Dumbarton,	-	-	5	Boghead Park.

After a protested game.

1882-83.

FIRST ROUND.	4 ;	Jordanhill,	-	-	0	Anniesland.
SECOND ROUND.	2 ;	Queen's Park,		-	3	Hampden Park.

1883-84.

Round.		Opponents.				Ground.
FIRST ROUND.	1 ;	Northern,	-	-	0	Springburn.
SECOND ROUND.	14 ;	Whitehill,	-	-	2	Kinning Park.
THIRD ROUND.	5 ;	Falkirk,	-	-	2	Kinning Park.
FOURTH ROUND.	6 ;	Dunblane,	-	-	1	Dunblane.
FIFTH ROUND.	3 ;	St. Bernard,	-	-	0	Edinburgh.
SIXTH ROUND.	5 ;	Cambuslang,	-	-	1	Cambuslang.
SEMI-FINAL.	0 ;	Vale of Leven,		-	3	Alexandria.

1884-85.

FIRST ROUND.	11 ;	Whitehill,	-	-	0	Kinning Park.
SECOND ROUND.	2 ;	Third Lanark,		-	2	Cathkin Park.
REPLAY.	0 ;	Third Lanark,		-	0	Kinning Park.
THIRD ROUND.	3 ;	Third Lanark,		-	0	Cathkin Park.
FOURTH ROUND.	8 ;	Arbroath,	-	-	1	Arbroath.

After protested game, which Arbroath won by 4-3.

FIFTH ROUND.	A Bye.					
SIXTH ROUND.	3 ;	Renton,	-	-	5	Renton.

1885-86.

FIRST ROUND.	0 ;	Clyde,	-	-	1	Barrowfield Park.

1886-87.

FIRST ROUND.	9 ;	Govan Athletic,		-	1	Kinning Park.
SECOND ROUND.	5 ;	Westbourne,	-	-	2	Kinning Park.
THIRD ROUND.	0 ;	Cambuslang,	-	-	2	Kinning Park.

1887-88.

FIRST ROUND.	4 ;	Battlefield,	-	-	1	Ibrox Park.
SECOND ROUND.	1 ;	Partick Thistle,		-	2	Partick.

1888-89.

FIRST ROUND.	4 ;	Partick Thistle,		-	2	Ibrox Park.
SECOND ROUND.	2 ;	Clyde,	-	-	2	Barrowfield Park.
REPLAY.	0 ;	Clyde,	-	-	3	Ibrox Park.

1889-90.

FIRST ROUND.	6 ;	United Abstainers,		2	Ibrox Park.
SECOND ROUND.	13 ;	Kelvinside Athletic,		0	Kelvinside.
THIRD ROUND.	0 ;	Vale of Leven,	-	0	Ibrox Park.
REPLAY.	2 ;	Vale of Leven,	-	3	Alexandria.

RANGERS' EVENTFUL YEARS

1890-91.

Round.		Opponents.			Ground.
FIRST ROUND.	0 ;	Celtic, -	-	- 1	Celtic Park.

1891-92.

FIRST ROUND.	5 ;	St. Bernards,		- 1	Ibrox Park.
SECOND ROUND	0 ;	Kilmarnock,		- 0	Ibrox Park.
REPLAY.	1 ;	Kilmarnock,		- 1	Kilmarnock.
REPLAY.	3 ;	Kilmarnock, -		- 2	Paisley.
THIRD ROUND.	2 ;	Annbank,	-	- 0	Ibrox Park.
FOURTH ROUND.	3 ;	Celtic, -	-	- 5	Celtic Park.

1892-93.

FIRST ROUND	7 ,	Annbank,	-	- 0	Ibrox Park
SECOND ROUND.	1 ,	Dumbarton, -		- 0	Dumbarton.
THIRD ROUND.	2 ;	St. Bernards,		- 3	Edinburgh

1893-94.

FIRST ROUND.	8 ,	Cowlairs,	-	- 0	Ibrox Park.
SECOND ROUND	2 ,	Leith Athletic,		- 0	Ibrox Park
THIRD ROUND.	5 ,	Clyde,	-	- 0	Barrowfield Park.
SEMI-FINAL.	1 ,	Queen's Park,		- 1	Ibrox Park.
REPLAY.	3 ,	Queen's Park,		- 1	Hampden Park
Final.	3 ;	**Celtic, -**	-	- **1**	**Hampden Park**

1894-95.

FIRST ROUND.	1 ;	Heart of Midlothian,	2	Ibrox Park.

1895-96.

FIRST ROUND.	1 ;	Dumbarton,	-	- 1	Dumbarton.
REPLAY.	3 ;	Dumbarton,	-	- 1	Ibrox Park.
SECOND ROUND.	5 ;	St. Mirren,	-	- 0	Ibrox Park.
THIRD ROUND.	2 ;	Hibernian,	-	- 3	Ibrox Park.

1896-97.

FIRST ROUND.	4 ;	Partick Thistle,		- 2	Inchview, Partick.
SECOND ROUND.	3 ;	Hibernian,	-	- 0	Ibrox Park.
THIRD ROUND.	4 ;	Dundee,	-	- 0	Carolina Park.
SEMI-FINAL.	7 ,	Morton,	-	- 2	Cappielow Park.
Final.	5 ;	**Dumbarton,**		- **1**	**Hampden Park.**

70

1897-98.

Round.		Opponents.				Ground.
FIRST ROUND.	8 ;	Polton Vale, -	-	0		Ibrox Park.
SECOND ROUND.	12 ;	Cartvale,	-	0		Ibrox Park.
THIRD ROUND.	3 ;	Queen's Park,	-	1		Ibrox Park.
SEMI-FINAL.	1 ;	Third Lanark,	-	1		Ibrox Park.
REPLAY.	2 ;	Third Lanark,	-	2		Cathkin Park.
REPLAY.	2 ;	Third Lanark,	-	0		Cathkin Park.
Final.	**2 ;**	**Kilmarnock,**	**-**	**0**		**Hampden Park.**

1898-99.

FIRST ROUND.	4 ;	Heart of Midlothian,		1		Ibrox Park.
SECOND ROUND.	4 ;	Ayr Parkhouse,	-	1		Ayr.
THIRD ROUND.	4 ;	Clyde, -	-	- 0		Ibrox Park
SEMI-FINAL.	2 ;	St. Mirren,	-	- 1		Paisley.
FINAL.	0 ;	Celtic, -	-	- 2		Hampden Park.

1899-1900.

FIRST ROUND.	4 ;	Morton, -	-	- 2		Ibrox Park.
SECOND ROUND.	12 ;	Maybole,	-	- 0		Ibrox Park.
THIRD ROUND.	6 ;	Partick Thistle,	-	1		Meadowside.
SEMI-FINAL.	2 ;	Celtic, -	-	- 2		Ibrox Park.
REPLAY.	0 ;	Celtic, -	-	- 4		Celtic Park.

1900-01.

FIRST ROUND.	0 ;	Celtic, -	-	- 1		Celtic Park.

1901-02.

FIRST ROUND.	6 ;	Johnstone,	-	- 1	Ibrox Park.
SECOND ROUND.	5 ;	Inverness Caledonian,	1		Ibrox Park.
THIRD ROUND.	2 ;	Kilmarnock,	-	0	Ibrox Park.
SEMI-FINAL.	0 ;	Hibernian,	-	- 2	Ibrox Park.

1902-03.

FIRST ROUND.	7 ;	Auchterarder Thistle,	0		Ibrox Park.
SECOND ROUND.	4 ;	Kilmarnock, -	- 0		Ibrox Park.
THIRD ROUND.	3 ;	Celtic, - -	- 0		Celtic Park.
SEMI-FINAL.	4 ;	Stenhousemuir,	- 1		Stenhousemuir.
Final.	**1 ;**	**Heart of Midlothian, 1**			**Celtic Park.**
Replay.	**0 ;**	**Heart of Midlothian, 0**			**Celtic Park.**
Replay.	**2 ;**	**Heart of Midlothian, 0**			**Celtic Park.**

RANGERS' EVENTFUL YEARS

1903-04.

Round.		Opponents.				Ground.
FIRST ROUND.	3 ;	Heart of Midlothian,			2	Ibrox Park.
SECOND ROUND.	2 ;	Hibernian,	-	-	1	Edinburgh.
THIRD ROUND.	1 ;	St. Mirren,	-	-	0	Paisley.
SEMI-FINAL.	3 ;	Morton,	-	-	0	Ibrox Park.
FINAL.	2 ;	Celtic, -	-	-	3	Hampden Park.

1904-05.

FIRST ROUND.	2 ;	Ayr Parkhouse,		-	1	Ibrox Park.
SECOND ROUND.	6 ;	Morton,	-	-	0	Greenock.
THIRD ROUND.	5 ;	Beith, -	-	-	1	Ibrox Park.
SEMI-FINAL.	2 ;	Celtic, -	-	-	0	Celtic Park.
FINAL.	0 ;	Third Lanark,	-	0	Hampden Park.
REPLAY.	1 ;	Third Lanark,	-	3	Hampden Park.

1905-06.

FIRST ROUND.	7 ;	Arthurlie,	-	-	1	Barrhead.
SECOND ROUND.	3 ;	Aberdeen,	-	-	2	Aberdeen.
THIRD ROUND.	0 ;	Port-Glasgow Ath.,		1	Port-Glasgow.

1906-07.

FIRST ROUND.	2 ;	Falkirk,	-	-	1	Falkirk.
SECOND ROUND.	4 ;	Galston,	-	-	0	Galston.
THIRD ROUND.	0 ;	Celtic, -	-	-	3	Ibrox Park.

1907-08.

FIRST ROUND.	2 ;	Falkirk,	-	-	2	Falkirk.
REPLAY.	4 ;	Falkirk,	-	-	1	Ibrox Park.
SECOND ROUND.	1 ,	Celtic, -	-	-	2	Ibrox Park.

1908-09.

FIRST ROUND.	3 ;	St. Johnstone,	-	0	Perth.
SECOND ROUND.	0 ;	Dundee,	-	-	0	Dundee.
REPLAY.	1 ;	Dundee,	-	-	0	Ibrox Park.
THIRD ROUND.	1 ;	Queen's Park,	-	0	Ibrox Park.
SEMI-FINAL.	1 ;	Falkirk, -	-	-	0	Falkirk.
FINAL	2 ;	Celtic, -	-	-	2	Hampden Park.
REPLAY.	1 ;	Celtic, -	-	-	1	Hampden Park.

Cup withheld.

72

1909-10.

Round.		Opponents.				Ground.
FIRST ROUND.	3 ;	Inverness Thistle,	-	-	1	Ibrox Park.
SECOND ROUND.	0 ;	Clyde,	-	-	2	Shawfield Park.

1910-11.

FIRST ROUND.	2 ;	Kilmarnock,	-	-	1	Ibrox Park.
SECOND ROUND.	3 ;	Morton,	-	-	0	Ibrox Park.
THIRD ROUND.	1 ;	Dundee,	-	-	2	Dundee.

1911-12.

FIRST ROUND.	3 ;	Stenhousemuir,	-	-	1	Ibrox Park.
SECOND ROUND.	1 ;	Clyde,	-	-	3	Shawfield Park.

1912-13.

FIRST ROUND.	A Bye.					
SECOND ROUND.	1 ;	Hamilton Acas.,	-	-	1	Hamilton.
REPLAY.	2 ;	Hamilton Acas.,	-	-	0	Ibrox Park.
THIRD ROUND.	1 ;	Falkirk,	-	-	3	Ibrox Park.

1913-14.

FIRST ROUND.	A Bye.					
SECOND ROUND.	5 ;	Alloa Athletic,	-	-	0	Ibrox Park.
THIRD ROUND.	1 ;	Hibernian,	-	-	2	Edinburgh.

1919-20.

FIRST ROUND.	0 ;	Dumbarton,	-	-	0	Ibrox Park.
REPLAY.	1 ;	Dumbarton,	-	-	0	Ibrox Park.
SECOND ROUND.	5 ;	Arbroath,	-	-	0	Ibrox Park.
THIRD ROUND.	3 ;	Broxburn United,	-	-	0	Ibrox Park.
FOURTH ROUND.	1 ;	Celtic,	-	-	0	Ibrox Park.
SEMI-FINAL.	1 ;	Albion Rovers,	-	-	1	Celtic Park.
REPLAY.	0 ;	Albion Rovers,	-	-	0	Celtic Park.
REPLAY.	0 ;	Albion Rovers,	-	-	2	Celtic Park.

73

RANGERS' EVENTFUL YEARS

1920-21.

Round.		Opponents.				Ground.
First Round.		A Bye.				
Second Round.	2 ;	Morton, -	-	-	0	Ibrox Park
Third Round.	0 ;	Alloa, -	-	-	0	Ibrox Park
Replay.	4 ;	Alloa, -	-	-	1	Ibrox Park
Fourth Round.	3 ;	Dumbarton, -	-	-	0	Dumbarton
Semi-Final.	4 ;	Albion Rovers,	-	-	1	Celtic Park
Final	0 ;	Partick Thistle,	-	-	1	Celtic Park

1921-22.

First Round	5 ;	Clachnacuddin,	-	-	0	Inverness
Second Round.	1 ;	Albion Rovers,	-	-	1	Coatbridge.
Replay	4 ;	Albion Rovers,	-	-	0	Ibrox Park
Third Round	4 ;	Heart of Midlothian,		-	0	Tynecastle.
Fourth Round.	1 ,	St Mirren,	-	-	1	Ibrox Park.
Replay.	2 ,	St Mirren,	-	-	0	Paisley.
Semi-Final.	2 ,	Partick Thistle,	-	-	0	Ibrox Park.
Final.	0 ;	Morton, -	-	-	1	Hampden Park.

1922-23.

First Round.	4 ,	Clyde, -	-	-	0	Shawfield Park.
Second Round.	0 ;	Ayr United, -	-	-	2	Ayr.

1923-24.

First Round.	4 ,	Lochgelly United,	-	-	1	Ibrox Park.
Second Round.	1 ;	St. Mirren,	-	-	0	Paisley.
Third Round.	1 ;	Hibernian,	-	-	2	Ibrox Park.

1924-25.

First Round.	3 ;	East Fife,	-	-	1	Methil.
Second Round.	2 ;	Montrose,	-	-	0	Montrose.
Third Round.	5 ;	Arbroath,	-	-	3	Ibrox Park.
Fourth Round.	2 ;	Kilmarnock,	-	-	1	Kilmarnock.
Semi-Final.	0 ;	Celtic, -	-	-	5	Hampden Park.

1925-26.

First Round.	3 ;	Lochgelly United,	-	-	0	Ibrox Park.
Second Round.	1 ;	Stenhousemuir,	-	-	0	Ibrox Park.
Third Round.	2 ;	Falkirk, -	-	-	0	Falkirk.
Fourth Round.	4 ;	Morton, -	-	-	0	Greenock.
Semi-Final.	0 ;	St. Mirren,	-	-	1	Celtic Park.

74

SCOTTISH CUP RECORD

1926-27.

Round.		Opponents.				Ground.
FIRST ROUND.	4 ;	Leith Athletic,	-	1		Leith.
SECOND ROUND.	6 ;	St. Mirren,	-	0		Ibrox Park
THIRD ROUND.	4 ;	Hamilton Acas.,	-	0		Ibrox Park.
FOURTH ROUND.	2 ;	Falkirk,	-	2		Falkirk.
REPLAY.*	0 ;	Falkirk, -	-	1		Ibrox Park.

* After extra time. McCandless went lame just at the end of 90 minutes and changed to outside left. Cunningham went to left back.

1927-28.

FIRST ROUND.	6 ;	East Stirlingshire,	-	0	Falkirk.
SECOND ROUND.	4 ;	Cowdenbeath,	-	2	Ibrox Park
THIRD ROUND.	3 ;	King's Park,	-	1	Ibrox Park.
FOURTH ROUND.	1 ;	Albion Rovers,	-	0	Coatbridge.
SEMI-FINAL.	3 ;	Hibernian,	-	0	Tynecastle.
Final.	**4 ;**	**Celtic, -**	-	**0**	**Hampden Park.**

1928-29.

FIRST ROUND.	11 ;	Edinburgh City,	-	1	Ibrox Park
SECOND ROUND.	5 ;	Partick Thistle,	-	1	Ibrox Park.
THIRD ROUND.	2 ;	Clyde,	-	0	Shawfield Park.
FOURTH ROUND.	3 ;	Dundee United,	-	1	Ibrox Park.
SEMI-FINAL.	3 ;	St. Mirren,	-	2	Hampden Park.
FINAL.	0 ;	Kilmarnock, -	-	2	Hampden Park.

1929-30.

FIRST ROUND.	1 ;	Queen's Park,	-	0	Hampden Park.
SECOND ROUND.	2 ;	Cowdenbeath,	-	2	Ibrox Park.
REPLAY.	3 ;	Cowdenbeath,	-	0	Cowdenbeath.
THIRD ROUND.	5 ;	Motherwell,	-	2	Motherwell.
FOURTH ROUND.	3 ;	Montrose,	-	0	Ibrox Park.
SEMI-FINAL.	4 ;	Heart of Midlothian,	1		Hampden Park.
Final.	**0 ;**	**Partick Thistle, -**		**0**	**Hampden Park.**
Replay.	**2 ;**	**Partick Thistle, -**		**1**	**Hampden Park.**

1930-31.

FIRST ROUND.	7 ;	Armadale,	-	1	Armadale.
SECOND ROUND.	1 ;	Dundee,	-	2	Ibrox Park.

RANGERS' EVENTFUL YEARS

1931-32.

Round.		Opponents.			Ground.
FIRST ROUND.	8 ;	Brechin City,	-	2	Ibrox Park.
SECOND ROUND.	5 ;	Raith Rovers,	-	0	Kirkcaldy.
THIRD ROUND.	1 ;	Heart of Midlothian,	0		Tynecastle.
FOURTH ROUND.	2 ,	Motherwell,	-	0	Ibrox Park.
SEMI-FINAL.	5 ;	Hamilton Acas.,	-	2	Celtic Park.
Final.	**1 ;**	**Kilmarnock,**	**-**	**1**	**Hampden Park.**
Replay.	**3 ;**	**Kilmarnock, -**	**-**	**0**	**Hampden Park.**

1932-33.

FIRST ROUND.	3 ;	Arbroath,	-	1	Ibrox Park.
SECOND ROUND.	1 ;	Queen's Park,	-	1	Ibrox Park.
REPLAY.	1 ;	Queen's Park,	-	1	Hampden Park.
REPLAY.	3 ;	Queen's Park,	-	1	Hampden Park.
THIRD ROUND.	0 ;	Kilmarnock, -	-	1	Kilmarnock.

1933-34.

FIRST ROUND.	14 ;	Blairgowrie,	-	2	Ibrox Park.
SECOND ROUND.	3 ;	Third Lanark,	-	0	Cathkin Park.
THIRD ROUND.	0 ,	Heart of Midlothian,	0		Ibrox Park.
REPLAY.	2 ;	Heart of Midlothian,	1		Tynecastle.
FOURTH ROUND.	1 ;	Aberdeen,	-	0	Ibrox Park.
SEMI-FINAL.	1 ;	St. Johnstone,	-	0	Hampden Park.
Final.	**5 ;**	**St. Mirren, -**	**-**	**0**	**Hampden Park.**

1934 - 35.

FIRST ROUND.	3 ;	Cowdenbeath,	-	1	Ibrox Park.
SECOND ROUND.	2 ;	Third Lanark, -	-	0	Ibrox Park.
THIRD ROUND.	1 ;	St. Mirren,	-	0	Ibrox Park.
FOURTH ROUND.	4 ;	Motherwell,	-	1	Motherwell.
SEMI-FINAL.	1 ;	Hearts,	-	1	Hampden.
REPLAY.	2 ;	Hearts,	-	0	Hampden.
Final.	**2 ;**	**Hamilton Acas.,**	**-**	**1**	**Hampden.**

1935 - 36.

FIRST ROUND.	3 ;	East Fife,	-	1	Ibrox.
SECOND ROUND.	3 ;	Albion Rovers, -	-	1	Coatbridge.
THIRD ROUND.	2 ;	St. Mirren,	-	1	Paisley.
FOURTH ROUND.	1 ;	Aberdeen,	-	0	Aberdeen.
SEMI-FINAL.	3 ;	Clyde,	-	0	Hampden.
Final.	**1 ;**	**Third Lanark,**	**-**	**0**	**Hampden.**

76

1936 - 37.

Round.	Opponents.			Ground.
FIRST ROUND.	0 ; Queen of the South,		1	Dumfries.

1937 - 38.

FIRST ROUND.	6 ; Alloa,	-	- 1	Alloa.
SECOND ROUND.	3 ; Queen of the South,		1	Ibrox.
THIRD ROUND.	A Bye.			
FOURTH ROUND.	2 ; Falkirk,	-	- 1	Falkirk.
SEMI-FINAL.	3 ; Kilmarnock,	-	- 4	Hampden.

1938 - 39.

FIRST ROUND.	1 ; Raith Rovers, -	-	- 0	Kirkcaldy.
SECOND ROUND.	2 ; Hamilton Acas.,		0	Ibrox.
THIRD ROUND.	1 ; Clyde,	-	- 4	Ibrox.

1946 - 47.

FIRST ROUND.	2 ; Clyde,	-	- 1	Ibrox.
SECOND ROUND.	0 ; Hibernian,	-	- 0	Ibrox.
REPLAY,	0 ; Hibernian,	-	- 2	Easter Road.

1947 - 48.

FIRST ROUND.	1 ; Stranraer,	-	- 0	Stranraer.
SECOND ROUND.	4 ; Leith Athletic,		- 0	Ibrox.
THIRD ROUND.	3 ; Partick Thistle,		- 0	Ibrox.
FOURTH ROUND.	1 ; East Fife,	-	- 0	Ibrox.
SEMI-FINAL.	1 ; Hibernian,	-	- 0	Hampden.
*Final.	1 ; Morton,	-	- 1	Hampden.
*Replay.	1 ; Morton,	-	- 0	Hampden.

* After extra time.

1948 - 49.

FIRST ROUND.	6 ; Elgin City,	-	- 1	Ibrox.
SECOND ROUND.	3 ; Motherwell,	-	- 0	Motherwell.
THIRD ROUND.	A Bye.			
FOURTH ROUND.	4 ; Partick Thistle,		- 0	Ibrox.
SEMI-FINAL.	3 ; East Fife,	-	- 0	Hampden.
Final.	4 ; Clyde,	-	- 1	Hampden.

77

1949- 50.

Round.	Opponents.			Ground.
FIRST ROUND.	4 ; Motherwell,	-	2	Motherwell.
SECOND ROUND.	8 ; Cowdenbeath,	-	o	Ibrox.
THIRD ROUND.	A Bye.			
FOURTH ROUND.	1 , Raith Rovers,	-	1	Ibrox.
REPLAY *	1 ; Raith Rovers,	-	1	Kirkcaldy.
REPLAY.	2 , Raith Rovers,	-	o	Ibrox.
SEMI-FINAL	1 ; Queen of the South,		1	Hampden.
REPLAY.	3 ; Queen of the South,		o	Hampden.
Final.	**3 ; East Fife,** -	-	**0**	**Hampden.**

*After extra time.

1950 - 51.

FIRST ROUND.	2 ; Queen of the South,	-	o	Ibrox.
SECOND ROUND.	2 ; Hibernian	-	- 3	Ibrox.

ANALYSIS OF SCOTTISH CUP RESULTS.

Only the undernoted Clubs have defeated Rangers in the Competition.

CLUB.				Played	Won.	Lost.	Goals.	
							For.	Agst.
CELTIC,	-	-	-	14	5	9	19	27*
DUMBARTON,	-	-	-	8	5	3	15	11
MORTON,		-	-	9	8	1	31	6
CLYDE,	-	-	-	13	8	5	37	15
PARTICK THISTLE,	-		-	12	10	2	37	10
QUEEN'S PARK,		-	-	8	6	2	15	11
THIRD LANARK,		-	-	8	6	2	14	6
HEARTS	-	-	-	9	8	1	24	8
HIBERNIAN,	-	-	-	10	4	6	15	15
FALKIRK,	-		-	8	6	2	17	9
VALE OF LEVEN,	-		-	4	0	4	4	14†
ST. BERNARDS,		-	-	3	2	1	10	4
DUNDEE, -	-	-	-	4	2	2	7	4
ALBION ROVERS,	-		-	5	4	1	12	4
CAMBUSLANG,	-	-	-	2	1	1	5	3
RENTON,	-	-	-	1	0	1	3	5
PORT-GLASGOW ATHLETIC,				1	0	1	0	1
AYR UNITED,	-	-	-	1	0	1	0	2
ST. MIRREN,	-	-	-	11	10	1	28	3
QUEEN OF THE SOUTH,		-		4	3	1	9	3
KILMARNOCK,	-		-	10	7	3	23	13

* In 1908-09 the Cup was withheld after Rangers and Celtic had played two drawn games in the Final.   That match is not included

† In 1878-79 the Cup was awarded Vale of Leven after a drawn match in the Final, which Rangers claimed to have won   That result is not included.

79

GLASGOW CUP RECORD.

1887-88.

Round.		Opponents.			Ground.
FIRST ROUND.	2 ;	Third Lanark,	-	2	Cathkin Park.
REPLAY.	2 ;	Third Lanark,	-	0	Ibrox Park.
SECOND ROUND.	3 ;	Pollokshields Ath.,		2	Pollokshields.
THIRD ROUND.	5 ;	Westbourne, -	-	1	Ibrox Park.
SEMI-FINAL.	0 ,	Cowlairs,	-	0	Gourlay Park.
REPLAY.	0 ;	Cowlairs,	-	0	Ibrox Park.
REPLAY.	2 ;	Cowlairs,	-	2	Cathkin Park.
REPLAY.	2 ;	Cowlairs,	-	1	Barrowfield Park.
REPLAY (after protest),	3 ;	Cowlairs,	-	1	Cathkin Park.
FINAL.	1 ;	Cambuslang, -	-	3	Hampden Park.

1888-89.

FIRST ROUND.	10 ;	United Abstainers, -		0	Ibrox Park.
SECOND ROUND.	7 ;	Pollokshields Ath.,		0	Pollokshields.
THIRD ROUND.	1 ;	Celtic, -	-	6	Ibrox Park.

1889-90.

FIRST ROUND.	5 ;	Pollokshaws,	-	1	Pollokshaws.
SECOND ROUND.	6 ;	Northern,	-	3	Springburn.
THIRD ROUND	1 ;	Third Lanark,	-	1	Cathkin Park.
REPLAY.	2 ;	Third Lanark,	-	0	Ibrox Park.
FOURTH ROUND.	0 ;	Queen's Park,	-	2	Ibrox Park.

1890-91.

FIRST ROUND.	12 ;	Carrington, -	-	2	Ibrox Park.
SECOND ROUND.	A Bye.				
THIRD ROUND.	3 ;	Third Lanark,	-	3	Cathkin Park.
REPLAY.	1 ;	Third Lanark,	-	1	Ibrox Park.
REPLAY.	3 ;	Third Lanark,	-	3	Cathkin Park.
REPLAY.	1 ;	Third Lanark,	-	3	Ibrox Park.

1891-92.

FIRST ROUND.	2 ;	Third Lanark,	-	0	Ibrox Park.
SECOND ROUND.	A Bye.				
THIRD ROUND.	0 ;	Queen's Park,	-	3	Ibrox Park.

1892-93.

Round.		Opponents.				Ground.
FIRST ROUND.	6 ;	Northern,	-	-	2	Ibrox Park.
SECOND ROUND.	3 ;	Linthouse,	-	-	2	Ibrox Park.
THIRD ROUND.	4 ;	Queen's Park,		-	2	Hampden Park.
SEMI-FINAL.	3 ;	Thistle, -	-	-	2	Braehead Park.
Final.	**3 ;**	**Celtic, -**	-	**-**	**1**	**Cathkin Park.**

1893-94.

FIRST ROUND.	W.O. ;	Whitefield.	Scratched.			
SECOND ROUND.	A Bye.					
THIRD ROUND.	11 ;	Pollokshaws, -		-	1	Ibrox Park.
SEMI-FINAL.	1 ;	Celtic, -	-	-	0	Ibrox Park.
Final.	**1 ;**	**Cowlairs,**	**-**	**-**	**0**	**Cathkin Park.**

1894-95.

FIRST ROUND.	2 ;	Queen's Park,		-	0	Ibrox Park.
SECOND ROUND.	3 ;	Third Lanark,		-	2	Ibrox Park.
SEMI-FINAL.	0 ;	Partick Thistle,		-	1	Inchview.
REPLAY (after protest),	5 ;	Partick Thistle, -			3	Inchview.
FINAL.	0 ;	Celtic, -	-	-	2	Cathkin Park.

1895-96.

FIRST ROUND.	2 ;	Queen's Park,		-	2	Hampden Park.
REPLAY.	2 ;	Queen's Park,		-	3	Ibrox Park.

1896-97.

FIRST ROUND.	5 ,	Third Lanark,		-	1	Ibrox Park.
SECOND ROUND.	A Bye.					
SEMI-FINAL.	3 ;	Linthouse,	-	-	0	Ibrox Park.
Final.	**1 ;**	**Celtic, -**	-	**-**	**1**	**Cathkin Park.**
Replay.	**2 ;**	**Celtic, -**	-	**-**	**1**	**Cathkin Park**

.1897-98.

FIRST ROUND.	6 ;	Partick Thistle,		-	0	Meadowside.
SECOND ROUND.	A Bye.					
SEMI-FINAL.	2 ;	Celtic, -	-	-	2	Ibrox Park.
REPLAY.	1 ;	Celtic, -	-	-	1	Ibrox Park.
REPLAY.	3 ;	Celtic, -	-	-	1	Ibrox Park.
Final.	**4 ;**	**Queen's Park,**		**-**	**0**	**Cathkin Park.**

F

1898-99.

Round.		Opponents.			Ground.
FIRST ROUND.	4 ;	Cameronians, -	-	0	Alexandra Park.
SEMI-FINAL	1 ,	Celtic, - -	-	1	Celtic Park.
REPLAY.	2 ,	Celtic, - -	-	1	Celtic Park.
FINAL.	0 ,	Queen's Park,	-	1	Cathkin Park.

1899-1900.

FIRST ROUND.	0 ,	Third Lanark,	-	0	Cathkin Park.
REPLAY.	5 ,	Third Lanark,	-	0	Ibrox Park
SEMI-FINAL.	7 ,	Queen's Park,	-	3	Ibrox Park
Final.	**1 ;**	**Celtic, - -**	**-**	**1**	**Cathkin Park.**
Replay.	**1 ;**	**Celtic, - -**	**-**	**0**	**Cathkin Park.**

1900-01.

FIRST ROUND.	3 ,	Celtic, - -	-	3	Celtic Park.
REPLAY.	4 ,	Celtic, - -	-	3	Ibrox Park.
SEMI-FINAL.	2 ,	Third Lanark,	-	1	Ibrox Park.
Final.	**3 ;**	**Partick Thistle,**	**-**	**1**	**Celtic Park.**

1901-02.

FIRST ROUND	5 ;	Normal Athletic,	-	0	Ibrox Park.
SECOND ROUND.	A Bye.				
SEMI-FINAL.	4 ;	Partick Thistle,	-	1	Ibrox Park.
Final.	**2 ;**	**Celtic, - -**	**-**	**2**	**Ibrox Park.**

Rangers awarded Cup, Celtic refusing to replay at Ibrox Park.

1902-03.

FIRST ROUND.	0 ;	Third Lanark,	-	1	Cathkin Park.

1903-04.

FIRST ROUND.	0 ;	Third Lanark,	-	2	Ibrox Park.

1904-05.

FIRST ROUND.	A Bye.				
SEMI-FINAL.	3 ;	Third Lanark,	-	0	Ibrox Park.
FINAL.	1 ,	Celtic, - -	-	2	Hampden Park.

1905-06.

FIRST ROUND.	0 ;	Clyde, - -	-	0	Shawfield Park.
REPLAY.	2 ;	Clyde, - -	-	1	Ibrox Park.
SECOND ROUND.	0 ;	Third Lanark,	-	0	Ibrox Park.
REPLAY.	1 ;	Third Lanark,	-	3	Cathkin Park.

1906-07.

Round.		Opponents.				Ground.
FIRST ROUND	2 ;	Queen's Park,		-	2	Hampden Park.
REPLAY.	0 ,	Queen's Park,		-	3	Ibrox Park.

1907-08.

FIRST ROUND.	4 ;	Clyde,	-	-	-	0	Shawfield Park.
SEMI-FINAL.	3 ;	Third Lanark,		-	0	Ibrox Park.
FINAL.	2 ,	Celtic,	-	-	-	2	Hampden Park.
REPLAY.	0 ,	Celtic,	-	-	-	0	Hampden Park.
REPLAY.	1 ,	Celtic,	-	-	-	2	Hampden Park

1908-09.

FIRST ROUND.	A Bye.					
SEMI-FINAL.	2 ;	Celtic,	- ' -	-	2	Celtic Park.
REPLAY.	0 ,	Celtic,	- -	-	2	Ibrox Park.

1909-1910.

FIRST ROUND.	2 ,	Partick Thistle,	-	1	Ibrox Park.
SEMI-FINAL.	2 ;	Third Lanark,	-	1	Cathkin Park.
Final.	**0 ;**	**Celtic, - -**	**-**	**1**	**Hampden Park.**

1910-11.

FIRST ROUND.	A Bye.					
SEMI-FINAL.	1 ;	Clyde,	- -	-	1	Shawfield Park.
REPLAY.	3 ;	Clyde,	- -	-	0	Ibrox Park
FINAL.	0 ;	Celtic,	- -	-	1	Hampden Park.

1911-12.

FIRST ROUND.	6 ,	Queen's Park,	-	1	Hampden Park.
SEMI-FINAL	1 ,	Clyde, - -	-	0	Ibrox Park
Final.	**1 ;**	**Partick Thistle,**	**- 0**	**Celtic Park.**

1912-13.

FIRST ROUND.	A Bye.					
SEMI-FINAL.	0 ;	Partick Thistle,	-	0	Firhill Park
REPLAY.	1 ,	Partick Thistle,	-	1	Ibrox Park.
REPLAY.	2 ,	Partick Thistle,	-	0	Firhill Park.
Final.	**3 ;**	**Celtic, - -**	**-**	**1**	**Hampden Park.**

1913-14.

FIRST ROUND.	A Bye.					
SEMI-FINAL.	1 ;	Clyde,	- -	-	0	Shawfield Park.
Final.	**3 ;**	**Third Lanark,**	**-**	**0**	**Hampden Park.**

83

RANGERS' EVENTFUL YEARS

1914-15.

Round.		Opponents.			Ground.
FIRST ROUND.	A Bye.				
SEMI-FINAL.	0 ,	Partick Thistle,	-	2	Ibrox Park.

1915-16.

FIRST ROUND.	4 ;	Queen's Park,	-	1	Hampden Park.
SEMI-FINAL.	7 ,	Partick Thistle,	-	2	Ibrox Park.
FINAL.	1 ;	Celtic, -	-	2	Hampden Park.

1916-17.

FIRST ROUND.	2 ;	Partick Thistle,	-	0	Firhill Park.
SEMI-FINAL.	0 ,	Celtic, -	-	3	Celtic Park.

1917-18.

FIRST ROUND (corners)	14 ;	Clyde (corners)		2	Shawfield Park.
SEMI-FINAL.	3 ;	Celtic, -	-	0	Celtic Park.
Final.	**4 ;**	**Partick Thistle,**	**-**	**1**	**Ibrox Park.**

1918-19.

FIRST ROUND.	A Bye.				
SEMI-FINAL.	3 ;	Queen's Park,	-	0	Ibrox Park.
Final.	**2 ;**	**Celtic, -**	**-**	**0**	**Hampden Park.**

1919-20.

FIRST ROUND.	0 ;	Celtic, -	-	1	Celtic Park.

1920-21.

FIRST ROUND.	2 ,	Queen's Park,	-	1	Hampden Park.
SEMI-FINAL.	1 ;	Celtic, -	-	2	Celtic Park.

1921-22.

FIRST ROUND.	A Bye.				
SEMI-FINAL.	2 ,	Third Lanark,	-	0	Cathkin Park.
Final.	**1 ;**	**Celtic, -**	**-**	**0**	**Hampden Park.**

1922-23.

FIRST ROUND.	3 ,	Partick Thistle,	-	1	Ibrox Park.
SEMI-FINAL.	2 ,	Third Lanark,	-	2	Cathkin Park.
REPLAY.	2 ;	Third Lanark,	-	1	Ibrox Park.
Final.	**0 ;**	**Clyde, -**	**-**	**0**	**Celtic Park.**
Replay.	**1 ;**	**Clyde, -**	**-**	**0**	**Celtic Park.**

1923-24.

Round.		Opponents.				Ground.
FIRST ROUND.	3 ;	Queen's Park,	-	-	0	Hampden Park.
SEMI-FINAL.	1 ;	Celtic,	-	-	0	Ibrox Park.
Final.	**3 ;**	**Third Lanark,**		**- 1**		**Ibrox Park.**

1924-25.

FIRST ROUND.	1 ;	Clyde,	-	-	0	Shawfield Park.
SEMI-FINAL.	0 ;	Partick Thistle,	-	-	0	Ibrox Park.
REPLAY.	2 ;	Partick Thistle,	-	-	0	Firhill Park.
Final.	**4 ;**	**Celtic,**	**-**	**- 1**		**Celtic Park.**

1925-26.

FIRST ROUND.	2 ;	Celtic,	-	-	2	Celtic Park.
REPLAY.	1 ;	Celtic,	-	-	1	Ibrox Park.
REPLAY.	0 ;	Celtic,	-	-	2	Ibrox Park.

1926-27.

FIRST ROUND.	4 ;	Third Lanark,		-	2	Ibrox Park.
SEMI-FINAL.	1 ;	Queen's Park,		-	1	Ibrox Park.
REPLAY.	3 ;	Queen's Park,		-	1	Hampden Park.
FINAL.	0 ;	Celtic,	-	-	1	Hampden Park.

1927-28.

SEMI-FINAL.	7 ;	Clyde,	-	-	0	Ibrox Park
FINAL.	1 ;	Celtic,	-	-	2	Hampden Park.

1928-29.

FIRST ROUND.	1 ;	Celtic,	-	-	2	Ibrox Park.

1929-30.

SEMI-FINAL.	2 ;	Partick Thistle,		-	0	Firhill Park.
Final.	**0 ;**	**Celtic,**	**-**	**- 0**		**Hampden Park.**
Replay.	**4 ;**	**Celtic,**	**-**	**- 0**		**Hampden Park.**

1930-31.

FIRST ROUND.	2 ;	Third Lanark,		-	1	Ibrox Park.
SEMI-FINAL.	1 ;	Queen's Park,		-	0	Ibrox Park.
FINAL.	1 ;	Celtic,	-	-	2	Hampden Park.

RANGERS' EVENTFUL YEARS

1931-32.

Round.		Opponents.				Ground.
FIRST ROUND	4 ,	Third Lanark,	-	1		Ibrox Park.
SEMI-FINAL.	1 ,	Celtic,	-	-	- 1	Celtic Park.
REPLAY.	2 ;	Celtic,	-	-	- 2	Ibrox Park.
REPLAY.	1 ;	Celtic,	-	-	- 0	Ibrox Park.
Final.	**3 ;**	**Queen's Park,**		-	**0**	**Hampden Park.**

1932-33.

FIRST ROUND.	6 ,	Queen's Park,	-	2	Hampden Park.
SEMI-FINAL.	4 ;	Third Lanark,	-	0	Ibrox Park.
Final.	**1 ;**	**Partick Thistle,**	-	**0**	**Hampden Park.**

1933-34.

SEMI-FINAL.	1 ;	Celtic,	-	-	- 1	Celtic Park.
REPLAY.	2 ,	Celtic,	-	-	- 1	Ibrox Park.
Final.	**2 ;**	**Clyde,**	-	-	**- 0**	**Hampden Park.**

1934 - 35.

SEMI-FINAL.	2 ;	Celtic,	-	-	- 1	Parkhead.
FINAL.	0 ,	Partick Thistle,		-	1	Hampden Park.

1935 - 36.

FIRST ROUND.	2 ;	Queen's Park,	-		- 0	Ibrox.
SEMI-FINAL.	2 ;	Clyde,	-		- 0	Ibrox.
Final.	**2 ;**	**Celtic,**	-		**- 0**	**Ibrox.**

1936 - 37.

FIRST ROUND.	4 ;	Queen's Park,	-		- 1	Ibrox.
SEMI-FINAL.	2 ;	Celtic,	-	-	- 1	Ibrox.
Final.	**2 ;**	**Partick Thistle,**	-		**- 2**	**Ibrox.**
Replay.	**6 ;**	**Partick Thistle,**			**- 1**	**Ibrox.**

1937 - 38.

FIRST ROUND.	3 ;	Clyde,	-	-	- 1	Shawfield.
SEMI-FINAL.	2 ;	Celtic,	-	-	- 1	Parkhead.
Final.	**2 ;**	**Third Lanark,**	-		**- 1**	**Hampden.**

1938 - 39.

Round.	Opponents.			Ground.
FIRST ROUND.	0 ; Queen's Park,	-	- 0	Hampden.
REPLAY.	2 , Queen's Park,	-	- 3	Ibrox.

1939 - 40.

FIRST ROUND.	4 ; Partick Thistle,	-	- 1	Firhill.
SEMI-FINAL.	2 ; Third Lanark,	-	- 2	Ibrox.
REPLAY.	2 ; Third Lanark,	-	- 1	Ibrox.
Final.	**3 ; Queen's Park,**	-	**- 1**	**Ibrox.**

1940 - 41.

FIRST ROUND.	5 ; Third Lanark,	-	- 2	Cathkin.
SEMI-FINAL.	1 ; Partick Thistle,	-	- 0	Ibrox.
Final.	**0 ; Celtic,**	- -	**- 1**	**Ibrox.**

1941 - 42.

SEMI-FINAL.	3 ; Celtic,	- -	- 2	Hampden.
Final.	**6 ; Clyde,**	- -	**- 0**	**Hampden.**

1942 - 43.

FIRST ROUND.	2 ; Celtic, -	-	- 1	Ibrox.
SEMI-FINAL.	2 ; Partick Thistle,	-	- 1	Firhill.
Final.	**5 ; Third Lanark,**	-	**- 2**	**Hampden.**

1943 - 44.

SEMI-FINAL.	3 ; Partick Thistle,	-	- 0	Firhill.
Final.	**2 ; Clyde,**	-	**- 0**	**Hampden.**

1944 - 45.

FIRST ROUND.	2 ; Partick Thistle,	-	- 1	Firhill.
SEMI-FINAL.	3 ; Queen's Park,	-	- 0	Hampden.
Final.	**3 ; Celtic,**	- -	**- 2**	**Hampden.**

1945 - 46.

FIRST ROUND.	3 ; Celtic,	- -	- 1	Ibrox.
SEMI-FINAL.	3 ; Clyde,	- - -	- 4	Shawfield.

RANGERS' EVENTFUL YEARS

1946 - 47.

Round.	Opponents.					Ground
SEMI-FINAL.	2 ; Clyde,	-	-	-	- 2	Shawfield.
REPLAY.	2 , Clyde,	-	-	-	- 4	Ibrox.

1947 - 48.

					Ground
FIRST ROUND.	1 ; Partick Thistle,	-	- 0	Ibrox.
SEMI-FINAL.	2 ; Queen's Park,	-	- 2	Hampden.
REPLAY, *	3 ; Queen's Park,	-	- 1	Ibrox.
Final.	**4 ; Third Lanark,**	-	**- 1**	**Hampden.**

* After extra time.

1948 - 49.

FIRST ROUND.	2 ; Clyde,	-	-	-	- 1	Shawfield.
SEMI-FINAL.	1 ; Third Lanark, -	-	- 4	Cathkin.

1949 - 50.

SEMI-FINAL.	2 ; Celtic,	-	-	-	- 1	Parkhead.
Final.	**2 ; Clyde,**	-	-	-	**- 2**	**Hampden.**
*Replay.	**2 ; Clyde,**	-	-	-	**- 1**	**Hampden.**

* After extra time.

1950 - 51.

SEMI-FINAL.	2 ; Partick Thistle,	-	- 2	Ibrox.
*REPLAY.	1 ; Partick Thistle,	-	- 1	Firhill.

* Thistle won on toss of coin after extra time.

GLASGOW CHARITY CUP RECORD.

1876-77.

Round.		Opponents.			
FINAL.	0 ,	Queen's Park, -	-	4	

1877-78.

FIRST ROUND.	1 ;	Third Lanark, -	-	2

1878-79.

FIRST ROUND.	4 ;	Third Lanark, -	-	1
Final.	**2 ;**	**Vale of Leven,**	**-**	**1**

1879-80.

FIRST ROUND.	3 ;	Dumbarton,	-	-	1
FINAL.	1 ;	Queen's Park, -	-	2	

1880-81.

FIRST ROUND.	8 ;	Dumbarton,	-	-	0
FINAL.	1 ;	Queen's Park, -	-	3	

1881-82.

FIRST ROUND	0 ;	Dumbarton,	-	-	4

1882-83.

FIRST ROUND.	3 ,	Vale of Leven,	-	2
FINAL.	1 ,	Queen's Park, -	-	4

1883-84.

FIRST ROUND.	1 ;	Queen's Park, -	-	2

1884-85.

FIRST ROUND.	0 ;	Dumbarton,	-	-	2

1885-86.

In a Qualifying Round, Vale of Leven beat
Rangers by 1 goal to 0.

1886-87.

Round.		Opponents.			
First Round.	4 ,	Cambuslang,	-	-	2
Second Round.	1 ,	Renton,	-	-	1
Replay.	1 ,	Renton,	-	-	1
Replay.	0 ,	Renton,	-	-	1

1887-88.

First Round.	3 ,	Vale of Leven,	-	-	3
Replay,	5 ,	Vale of Leven,	-	-	3
Second Round.	1 ;	Renton,	-	-	5

In **1888-89** and in **1889-90**.
Rangers did not compete.

1890-91.

Rangers, Celtic and Third Lanark did **not**
compete owing to pressure of League **Matches**.

1891-92.

First Round.	7 ,	Queen's Park,	-	-	1
Final.	0 ,	Celtic,	-	-	2

1892-93.

First Round.	3 ;	Third Lanark,	-	-	2
Final.	0 ,	Celtic,	-	-	5

1893-94.

First Round.	0 ;	Queen's Park,	-	-	2

1894-95.

First Round.	4 ;	Third Lanark,	-	-	0
Final.	0 ,	Celtic,	-	-	4

1895-96.

First Round.	1 ;	Celtic,	-	-	6

1896-97.

First Round.	4 ;	Celtic,	-	-	1
Final.	**6 ;**	**Third Lanark,**		**-**	**1**

GLASGOW CHARITY CUP RECORD

1897-98.

Round.	Opponents.		
FIRST ROUND.	2 ; Celtic, - -	-	o
FINAL.	o , Third Lanark, -	-	I

1898-99.

FIRST ROUND.	4 , Third Lanark, -	-	I
Final.	**0 ; Celtic, - -**	**-**	**2**

1899-1900.

FIRST ROUND.	2 ; Third Lanark, -	-	o
Final.	**5 ; Celtic, - -**	**-**	**1**

1900-01.

FIRST ROUND.	o ; Celtic, - -	-	o
REPLAY.	o ; Celtic, - -	-	I

1901-02

FIRST ROUND.	o ; Hibernian, -	-	I

1902-03.

FIRST ROUND.	o ; St. Mirren, -	-	I

1903-04.

FIRST ROUND.	I ; Third Lanark, -	-	o
Final.	**5 ; Celtic,**	**-**	**2**

1904-05.

FIRST ROUND.	o ; Partick Thistle,	-	5

1905-06.

FIRST ROUND.	A Bye.		
SECOND ROUND.	5 ; Celtic, - -	-	3
Final.	**3 ; Queen's Park,**	**-**	**2**

1906-07.

Round.		Opponents.		
FIRST ROUND.	3 ;	Partick Thistle,	-	o
SECOND ROUND.	1 ;	Third Lanark, -	-	o
Final.	**1 ;**	**Celtic,** - -	-	**0**

1907-08.

FIRST ROUND	3 ;	Third Lanark, -	-	1
SECOND ROUND.	1 ;	Queen's Park, -	-	3

1908-09.

FIRST ROUND	3 ,	Partick Thistle,	-	1
SECOND ROUND.	3 ,	Third Lanark, -	-	2
Final.	**4 ;**	**Celtic,** - -	-	**2**

1909-10.

FIRST ROUND.	A Bye			
SECOND ROUND.	o ;	Clyde, - -	-	1

1910-11.

FIRST ROUND.	3 ;	Clyde, - -	-	2
SECOND ROUND.	1 ;	Queen's Park, -	-	o
Final.	**2 ;**	**Celtic,** - -	-	**1**

1911-12.

FIRST ROUND.	1 ;	Third Lanark, -	-	o
SECOND ROUND.	1 ,	Clyde, - -	-	2

1912-13.

FIRST ROUND.	A Bye.			
SECOND ROUND.	3 ;	Partick Thistle,	-	1
Final.	**2 ;**	**Celtic,** - -	-	**3**

1913-14.

FIRST ROUND.	2 ;	Clyde, - -	-	1
SECOND ROUND.	1 ;	Third Lanark, -	-	1
	(3 corners)		(4 corners)	

1914-15.

Round.	Opponents.				
FIRST ROUND.	A Bye				
SECOND ROUND.	3 ; Third Lanark, -	-			0
FINAL.	0 , Celtic,	-	-	-	2

1915-16.

FIRST ROUND.	A Bye.				
SECOND ROUND.	0 ; Celtic,	-	-	-	3

1916-17.

FIRST ROUND.	A Bye.				
SECOND ROUND.	0 ; Celtic,	-	-	-	2

1917-18.

FIRST ROUND.	0 ; Partick Thistle,		-	2

1918-19.

FIRST ROUND.	3 ; Third Lanark, -	-			0
SECOND ROUND.	2 ; Celtic,	-	-	-	0
Final.	**2 ; Queen's Park,**		-		**1**

1919-20.

FIRST ROUND.	4 ; Partick Thistle,		-		0
SECOND ROUND.	1 ; Celtic,	-	-	-	2

1920-21.

FIRST ROUND.	5 ; Queen's Park, -	-			0
SECOND ROUND.	2 ; Clyde,	-	-	-	0
FINAL.	0 ; Celtic,	-	-	-	2

1921-22.

SEMI-FINAL.	10 corners ; Celtic, corners, 6
Final.	**3 goals ; Queen's Park, 1 goal.**

1922-23.

SEMI-FINAL.	1 ; Celtic,	-	-	-	0
Final.	**4 ; Queen's Park,**		-		**0**

1923-24.

Round.		Opponents.			Ground.
FIRST ROUND.	3 ,	Clyde, - -	-	o	Celtic Park.
SEMI-FINAL.	1 ,	Partick Thistle,	-	o	Ibrox Park.
Final.	**1 ;**	**Celtic,** - -	-	**2**	**Hampden Park.**

1924-25.

FIRST ROUND.	4 ,	Third Lanark,	-	1	Ibrox Park.
SEMI-FINAL.	2 ;	Partick Thistle,	-	1	Hampden Park.
Final.	**1 ;**	**Clyde,** - -	-	**0**	**Ibrox Park.**

1925-26.

FIRST ROUND.	3 ;	Clyde, - -	-	4	Ibrox Park.

1926-27.

FIRST ROUND	8 ,	Queen's Park,	-	1	Ibrox Park.
SEMI-FINAL.	4 ,	Celtic, - -	-	1	Celtic Park.
FINAL	3 ,	Partick Thistle,	-	6	Hampden Park

1927-28.

SEMI-FINAL.	2 ,	Celtic, - -	-	o	Celtic Park
Final.	**3 ;**	**Queen's Park,**	-	**1**	**Celtic Park.**

1928-29.

FIRST ROUND	2 ,	Partick Thistle,	-	1	Ibrox Park.
SEMI-FINAL.	2 ,	Third Lanark,	-	1	Firhill Park.
		After extra time.			
Final.	**4 ;**	**Celtic,** - -	-	**2**	**Ibrox Park.**

1929-30.

FIRST ROUND	2 ;	Partick Thistle,	-	1	Firhill Park
SEMI-FINAL.	5 ,	Third Lanark,	-	1	Ibrox Park.
Final.	**2 ;**	**Celtic,** - -	-	**2**	**Hampden Park.**

The game was still drawn after extra time   The clubs
then tossed, and Rangers won

1930-31.

FIRST ROUND	2 ;	Celtic, - -	-	2	Hampden Park

After extra time Rangers won by three corners to two.

SEMI-FINAL.	1 ,	Partick Thistle,	-	o	Ibrox Park.
Final.	**2 ;**	**Queen's Park,**	-	**1**	**Hampden Park.**

After extra time.

GLASGOW CHARITY CUP RECORD

1931-32.

Round.		Opponents.			Ground.
SEMI-FINAL.	3 ;	Queen's Park,	-	1	Ibrox Park.
Final.	**6 ;**	**Third Lanark,**	**-**	**1**	**Hampden Park.**

1932-33.

FIRST ROUND.	3 ,	Third Lanark,	-	1	Ibrox Park.
SEMI-FINAL.	2 ,	Partick Thistle,	-	0	Ibrox Park.
Final.	**1 ;**	**Queen's Park,**	**-**	**0**	**Hampden Park.**

1933-34.

SEMI-FINAL.	1 ;	Partick Thistle,	-	1	Ibrox Park.

After extra time, Rangers won by 7 corners to 4.

Final.	**1 ;**	**Celtic, -**	**-**	**0**	**Hampden Park.**

1934 - 35.

FIRST ROUND.	3 ;	Third Lanark,	-	1	Ibrox.
SEMI-FINAL.	0 ;	Partick Thistle,	-	1	Firhill.

1935 - 36.

FIRST ROUND.	1 ;	Third Lanark,	-	0	Ibrox.
SEMI-FINAL,	1 ;	Clyde,	-	0	Shawfield.
Final.	**2 ;**	**Celtic,**	**-**	**4**	**Hampden.**

1936 - 37.

FIRST ROUND.	0 ;	Queen's Park,	-	3	Hampden.

1937 - 38.

FIRST ROUND.	4 ;	Clyde,	-	1	Ibrox.
SEMI-FINAL.	1 ;	Third Lanark,	-	0	Ibrox.
Final.	**0 ;**	**Celtic,**	**-**	**2**	**Hampden.**

1938 - 39.

SEMI-FINAL.	2 ;	Queen's Park,	-	1	Ibrox.
Final.	**0 ,**	**Third Lanark,**	**-**	**0**	**Hampden.**

(7 corners)   (4 corners)

1939 - 40.

SEMI-FINAL.	5 ;	Celtic,	-	1	Ibrox.
Final. (7 corners)	**1 ;**	**Clyde,** (2 corners)	**1**		**Hampden.**

1940 - 41.

SEMI-FINAL.	3 ;	Third Lanark,	-	1	Ibrox.
Final.	**3 ;**	**Partick Thistle,**	**0**		**Hampden.**

RANGERS' EVENTFUL YEARS

1941 - 42.

Round.	Opponents.		Ground.
SEMI-FINAL.	2 ; Celtic, - - 1	Hampden.
Final.	**3 ; Clyde, - - 1**	**Hampden.**

1942 - 43.

FIRST ROUND.	1 ; Clyde, - - 2	Ibrox.

1943 : 44.

SEMI-FINAL.	3 ; Partick Thistle, - 0	Ibrox.
Final.	**2 ; Clyde, - - 1**	**Hampden.**

1944 - 45.

FIRST ROUND.	1 ; Queen's Park, - 0	Ibrox.
SEMI-FINAL.	4 ; Clyde, - - 0	Ibrox.
Final.	**2 ; Celtic, - - 1**	**Hampden.**

1945 - 46.

FIRST ROUND.	4 ; Queen's Park, - 1	Ibrox.
SEMI-FINAL.	3 ; Celtic, - - 1	Celtic Park.
Final.	**2 ; Third Lanark, - 0**	**Hampden.**

1946 - 47.

SEMI-FINAL.	4 ; Partick Thistle, - 0	Ibrox.
Final.	**1 ; Celtic, - - 0**	**Ibrox.**

1947 - 48.

SEMI-FINAL.	3 ; Partick Thistle, - 0	Ibrox.
Final.	**2 ; Celtic, - - 0**	**Hampden.**

1948 - 49.

SEMI-FINAL.	0 ; Partick Thistle, - 1	Ibrox.

1949 - 50.

SEMI-FINAL.	4 ; Partick Thistle, - 0	Ibrox.
Final.	**0 ; Celtic, - - 3**	**Hampden.**

1950-51.

FIRST ROUND.	2 ; Celtic, - - - 1	Hampden Park.
SEMI-FINAL.	1 ; Third Lanark, - 1	*Hampden Park.
Final.	**2 : Partick Thistle, - 0**	**Hampden Park.**

* Won on toss of coin.

96

WAR SCOTTISH CUP.

1939 - 40.

Round.		Opponents.					Ground.
FIRST ROUND.	2 ;	Alloa,	-		-	2	Ibrox.
FIRST ROUND.	4 ;	Alloa,	-		-	1	Alloa.
SECOND ROUND.	3 ;	Falkirk,	-		-	2	Ibrox.
SECOND ROUND.	0 ;	Falkirk,	-		-	0	Falkirk.
THIRD ROUND.	3 ;	St. Mirren,			-	1	Ibrox.
SEMI-FINAL.	4 ;	Motherwell,			-	1	Hampden.
Final.	**1 ;**	**Dundee United,**				**0**	**Hampden.**

SOUTHERN LEAGUE CUP.

1940 - 41.

	Opponents.				Ground.
6 ;	Dumbarton, -		-	3	Ibrox.
8 ;	Dumbarton, -		-	1	Dumbarton.
4 ;	Falkirk,	-	-	0	Ibrox.
0 ;	Falkirk,	-	-	2	Falkirk.
2 ,	Third Lanark,		-	0	Ibrox.
2 ;	Third Lanark,		-	1	Cathkin.

Semi-Final.

4 ;	St. Mirren, -		-	1	Hampden.

Final.

1 ;	**Hearts, -**		**-**	**1**	**Hampden.**
4 ;	**Hearts, -**		**-**	**2**	**Hampden.**

1941 - 42.

5 ;	Third Lanark,		-	1	Ibrox.
5 ;	Third Lanark,		-	2	Cathkin.
3 ;	Motherwell, -		-	1	Motherwell.
3 ;	Motherwell, -		-	0	Ibrox.
2 ;	Hearts,	-	-	1	Ibrox.
2 ;	Hearts,	-	-	1	Tynecastle.

Semi-Final.

2 ;	Celtic,	-	-	0	Hampden.

Final.

1 ;	**Morton,**	-	**-**	**0**	**Hampden.**

97

G

1942 - 43.

	Opponents.				Ground.
3 ;	St. Mirren,	-	-	0	Paisley.
3 ,	Celtic, -	-	-	0	Ibrox.
2 ,	Hibernian,		-	0	Edinburgh.
3 ,	St. Mirren,	-	-	1	Ibrox.
2 ;	Celtic, -	-	-	0	Parkhead
1 ;	Hibernian,	-	-	0	Ibrox.

Semi-Final.

3 ;	Hamilton Acas ,	-	0	Hampden.

Final.

1 ; Falkirk,   -   -   1   Hampden.
(11 corners)   (3 corners)

1943 - 44.

4 ;	Airdrieonians,		-	0	Ibrox.
1 ;	Airdrieonians,		-	0	Airdrie.
2 ;	Hearts,	-	-	0	Ibrox.
4 ;	Hearts,	-	-	2	Tynecastle.
0 ,	Motherwell,	-	-	1	Ibrox.
3 ,	Motherwell,	-	-	2	Motherwell.

Semi-Final.

4 ;	Celtic, -	-	-	2	Hampden.

Final.

0 ;	Hibernian,	-	-	0	Hampden.

(5 corners)   (6 corners)

1944 - 45.

2 ;	Albion Rovers,	-	1	Ibrox.
3 ,	Albion Rovers,	-	1	Coatbridge.
2 ;	Hibernian,	-	-	0	Ibrox.
1 ;	Hibernian,	-	-	1	Easter Road.
2 ;	Third Lanark,	-	0	Ibrox.
4 ;	Third Lanark,	-	2	Cathkin.

Semi-Final.

3 ;	Queen's Park,	-	0	Hampden.

Final.

2 ; Motherwell,   -   1   Hampden.

98

1945 - 46.

	Opponents.		Ground.
4 ;	Queen of the South,	o	Ibrox.
2 ;	Queen of the South,	o	Dumfries.
4 ;	Motherwell, - -	2	Ibrox.
3 ;	Motherwell, - -	o	Motherwell.
1 ;	Morton, - -	o	Ibrox.
1 ;	Morton, - -	1	Greenock.

Quarter Final.

3 ;	Dundee,	- -	1	Hampden.

Semi-Final.

*2 ;	Hearts,	- -	1	Hampden.

Final.

2 ;	Aberdeen,	-	3	Hampden.

* After extra time.

SCOTTISH VICTORY CUP.

1945 - 46.

Round.	Opponents.			Ground.
First Round.	4 ; Stenhousemuir, -	1		Ibrox
First Round.	4 ; Stenhousemuir, -	1		Stenhousemuir.
Second Round.	4 ; Airdrieonians, -	o		Airdrie.
Third Round.	1 , Falkirk, - -	1		Falkirk.
Replay.	2 ; Falkirk, - -	o		Ibrox.
Semi-Final.	o ; Celtic, - -	o		Hampden.
Replay.	2 ; Celtic, - -	o		Hampden.
Final.	**3 ; Hibernian, -**	**1**		**Hampden.**

SCOTTISH LEAGUE CUP.

1946 - 47.

	Opponents.			Ground.
4 ;	St. Mirren, -	-	0	Ibrox.
4 ;	St. Mirren, -	-	0	Paisley.
1 ;	Queen's Park,	-	0	Ibrox.
4 ,	Queen's Park,	-	2	Hampden.
3 ,	Morton,	-	0	Ibrox.
2 ,	Morton,	-	0	Greenock.

Quarter Final.

2 ;	Dundee United,	-	1	Ibrox.
1 ,	Dundee United,	-	1	Dundee.

Semi-Final.

3 ;	Hibernian,	-	1	Hampden.

Final.

4 ; Aberdeen,   - 0 Hampden.

1947 - 48.

2 ,	Celtic, -	-	0	Ibrox
0 ,	Celtic, -	-	2	Parkhead.
3 ,	Dundee,	-	0	Ibrox.
1 ,	Dundee,	-	1	Dundee.
3 ,	Third Lanark,	-	0	Ibrox.
3 ,	Third Lanark,	-	1	Cathkin.

Quarter Final.

2 ;	Stenhousemuir,	-	0	Ibrox.

Semi-Final.

0 ,	Falkirk,	-	1	Hampden.

1948 - 49.

2 ;	Celtic, -	-	1	Ibrox.
1 ,	Celtic, -	-	3	Parkhead.
1 ;	Clyde, -	-	1	Ibrox.
3 ;	Clyde, -	-	1	Shawfield.
1 ;	Hibernian,	-	0	Ibrox.
0 ;	Hibernian,	-	0	Easter Road.

Quarter Final.

1 ;	St. Mirren, -	-	0	Ibrox.

Semi-Final.

4 ;	Dundee,	-	1	Hampden.

Final.

2 ; Raith Rovers, - 0 Hampden.

1949 - 50.

Opponents.					Ground.
4 ;	Aberdeen,	-	-	2	Ibrox.
1 ;	Aberdeen,	-	-	1	Aberdeen.
2 ;	Celtic, -	-	-	0	Ibrox.
2 ;	Celtic, -	-	-	3	Parkhead.
5 ;	St. Mirren, -	-	-	1	Ibrox.
1 ;	St. Mirren, -	-	-	1	Paisley.

Quarter Final.

2 ;	Cowdenbeath,	-	3	Ibrox.
*3 ;	Cowdenbeath,	-	1	Cowdenbeath.

Semi-Final.

*1 ;	East Fife,	-	-	2	Hampden.

* After extra time.

1950 - 51.

1 ;	Aberdeen,	-	-	2	Ibrox.
0 ;	Aberdeen,	-	-	2	Aberdeen.
4 ;	Clyde,	-	-	0	Ibrox.
5 ;	Clyde, -	-	-	1	Shawfield.
6 ;	Morton,	-	-	1	Ibrox.
2 ;	Morton,	-	-	1	Greenock.

Rangers failed to qualify for Quarter Final.

RANGERS' INTERNATIONALISTS.

	E.	W.	I.	E.L.	I.L.	L. of I.	Total
A. Archibald, -	4	3	1	7	3	—	18
J. B. Barker, -	—	2	—	1	1	—	4
A. Bennett, -	3	5	3	6	1	—	18
J. Bowie, - -	1	—	1	1	1	—	4
Geo. Brown, -	6	6	2	4	1	—	19
R. Brown, -	—	—	2	3	1	—	6
J. Buchanan, -	2	—	—	—	—	—	2
T. Cairns, - -	3	3	2	5	1	—	14
J. Cameron, -	—	—	1	—	—	—	1
J. Campbell, -	1	1	2	1	—	—	5
P. Campbell, -	—	2	—	—	—	—	2
W. Chalmers, -	—	—	1	—	—	—	1
W. Cheyne, -	—	—	—	—	1	—	1
S. Cox, - -	3	1	1	2	3	2	12
T. Craig, - -	1	1	3	3	2	—	10
D. Crawford, -	—	2	1	1	—	—	4
A. Cunningham, -	5	3	4	7	3	—	22
J Dawson, -	3	2	4	3	6	1	19
M. Dickie, - -	—	1	2	1	—	—	4
J. Drummond, -	6	1	7	3	—	—	17
J. Duncan, -	—	2	—	—	—	—	2
J. Duncanson, -	—	—	1	—	—	1	2
J. Fleming, -	1	—	—	1	—	—	2

	E.	W.	I.	E.L.	I.L.	L. of I.	Total
J. H. Galt, -	—	1	1	1	—	—	3
N. Gibson, - -	6	2	6	8	2	—	24
W. Gibson, -	—	—	—	—	1	—	1
G. Gillespie, -	2	4	1	—	—	—	7
T. Gillick, - -	—	1	1	2	2	—	6
J. Gordon, - -	4	2	4	4	4	—	18
J. Gossland, -	—	—	1	—	—	—	1
D. Gow, - -	1	—	—	—	—	—	1
J. R. Gow, -	—	—	1	—	—	—	1
J. Graham, -	—	—	—	—	1	—	1
D. Gray, - -	1	4	3	4	2	—	14
D. Haddow, -	1	—	—	1	—	—	2
R. C. Hamilton, -	3	4	4	5	2	—	18
T. Hamilton, -	1	—	—	—	—	—	1
C. Heggie, - -	—	—	1	—	—	—	1
G. Henderson (H.B)	—	—	1	—	—	—	1
G. Henderson (F.),	—	—	—	—	1	—	1
D. Hill, - -	1	2	—	—	—	—	3
T. Hyslop, - -	2	—	—	—	—	—	2
J. Inglis, - -	1	1	—	—	—	—	2
D. Kinnear, -	—	—	—	2	—	—	2
A. Kyle, - -	—	—	—	2	—	—	2
G. Law, -	1	1	1	—	—	—	3
G. Livingston, -	2	1	—	1	—	—	4
J. L. Logan, -	—	—	—	1	—	—	1

	E.	W.	I.	E.L.	I.L.	L. of I.	Total
T. P. Low, -	—	—	1	1	—	—	2
R. Macaulay, -	—	—	1	1	—	—	2
I. McColl, - -	1	1	1	—	—	—	3
A. McCreadie, -	1	1	—	—	—	—	2
H. McCreadie, -	—	—	—	1	—	—	1
H. McHardy, -	—	—	1	—	—	—	1
H. McIntyre, -	—	1	—	—	—	—	1
J. McIntyre, -	—	1	—	—	—	—	1
R. McKay, -	—	1	—	—	1	—	2
M. McNeil, -	1	1	—	—	—	—	2
R. McPhail, -	5	3	5	5	1	—	19
J. McPherson, -	4	2	2	3	2	—	13
R. Main, - -	—	1	—	3	3	—	7
J. Marshall, -	3	—	—	1	—	—	4
R. Marshall, -	—	—	2	1	—	—	3
J. May, - -	1	2	2	3	—	—	8
D. D. Meiklejohn,	4	5	5	5	1	—	20
J. Miller, - -	2	1	—	2	1	—	6
D. Mitchell, -	3	—	2	2	—	—	7
A. L. Morton, -	11	10	9	11	2	—	43
T. Muirhead, -	1	3	4	4	2	—	14
R. G. Neill, -	—	2	—	1	—	—	3
W. G. Nicholson,	—	—	—	1	—	—	1
J. Oswald, - -	2	1	—	3	—	—	6
W. Reid, - -	3	2	4	4	2	—	15

	E.	W.	I.	E.L.	I.L.	L. of I.	Total
W. Robb, - -	—	2	—	—	2	—	4
J. Robertson, -	7	6	3	5	1	—	22
E. Rutherford, -	—	—	—	—	1	—	1
J. Shaw, - -	2	—	—	1	1	—	4
J. Simpson, -	3	4	4	3	1	—	15
A. Smith, - -	7	6	7	10	3	—	33
J. Smith, - -	—	—	2	—	—	—	2
N. Smith, - -	4	4	4	6	3	—	21
F. Speedie, -	1	1	1	1	—	—	4
J. Speirs, - -	—	1	—	—	—	—	1
J. Stark, - -	1	—	1	2	—	—	4
W. Thornton, -	1	1	2	1	—	—	5
T. Vallance, -	4	3	—	—	—	—	7
A. Venters, -	2	—	1	3	1	—	7
W. Waddell, -	3	2	2	1	2	—	10
J. Walker, - -	—	2	3	4	1	—	10
J. Watson, -	—	1	—	—	—	—	1
W. Woodburn, -	4	3	3	3	2	1	16
T. Wylie, - -	—	—	1	—	—	—	1
G. Young, - -	5	3	5	5	4	4	26
Totals,	151	135	141	177	76	9	689

AGAINST CONTINENTALS.

Austria : 1933—D. Meiklejohn, G. Brown, R. M McPhail. 1937—J. Dawson, J. Simpson. 1950—G. Young, W. Woodburn. 1951—G. Young, S. Cox, W. Woodburn, W. Waddell.

Belgium :—1946—J. Shaw. 1947—G. Young, J. Shaw, W. Woodburn 1948—G. Young 1951—G. Young, S. Cox, I. McColl, W. Woodburn, W. Waddell.

Czechoslovakia : 1937—J. Dawson, J. Simpson, G. Brown, R. McPhail. 1938—G. Brown, D. Kinnear.

Denmark :—1951—G Young, S Cox, W. Woodburn, W. Waddell.

France :—1932—R McPhail, A. L. Morton 1948—G Young, S Cox, E. Rutherford 1949—G. Young, S. Cox, W. Woodburn, W. Waddell, W. Thornton. 1950—G Young, S Cox, W. Woodburn, I. McColl 1951—G. Young, S Cox, W. Woodburn, W Waddell.

Germany : — 1936 — J. Dawson, J. Simpson, G. Brown, R. McPhail.

Holland :—1938—J. Dawson, G. Brown, J. McKillop

Hungary :—1930—J. Dawson, Scott Symon.

Luxembourg :—1947—G. Young, J. Shaw, W. Woodburn

Portugal :—1950—G. Young, S. Cox, W. Woodburn

Switzerland :—1946—R. Brown, J. Shaw, W Waddell, W. Thornton. 1950—G. Young, S Cox.

Gillick was with Everton when he played against Austria and Czechoslovakia in 1937 and against Hungary in 1939. R Brown was with Queen's Park when he played against Belgium in 1946.

OUR IRISH INTERNATIONALS.

Alec Craig : England, 1908, 1914 ; Scotland, 1908, 1909, 1912, 1914 ; Wales, 1908, 1912, 1914.

Robert Manderson : England, 1925 ; Scotland, 1920, 1925, 1926 Wales, 1920.

William McCandless : England, 1920, 1921 ; Scotland, 1922, 1924 ; Wales, 1920, 1924, 1929.

Robert Hamilton : England, 1929, 1930 , Scotland, 1928, 1930, 1932.

Robert McDonald : England, 1932 ; Scotland, 1930

Sam English : Wales, 1932.

William Simpson : England, Wales and France, 1950-51 ; English League and League of Ireland, 1949-50 ; Scottish League and English League, 1950-51.

Grand Total,   -   -   **759**

106

ANALYSIS OF RANGERS' LEAGUE RESULTS.

(Compiled to end of Season 1950-51).

CLUB	Played	Won	Drawn	Lost	Goals For	Goals Agst	Points For	Points Agst
CELTIC,	108	42	36	30	169	150	120	96
HEART OF MIDLOTHIAN,	108	61	19	28	197	137	141	75
THIRD LANARK,	96	66	15	15	240	112	147	45
ST. MIRREN,	106	70	24	12	285	113	164	48
DUNDEE,	94	58	17	19	225	111	133	55
HIBERNIAN,	94	60	18	16	209	97	138	50
CLYDE,	88	65	15	8	253	85	145	31
PARTICK THISTLE,	90	62	15	13	217	85	139	41
KILMARNOCK,	82	62	11	9	224	72	135	29
MORTON,	72	54	9	9	180	64	117	27
QUEEN'S PARK,	80	59	12	9	205	68	130	30
MOTHERWELL,	82	54	17	11	176	84	125	39
AIRDRIEONIANS,	70	44	9	17	165	90	97	43
FALKIRK,	76	48	16	12	171	78	112	40
HAMILTON ACAS.,	68	48	11	9	179	67	107	29
ABERDEEN,	74	42	21	11	144	70	105	43
DUMBARTON,	30	20	4	6	73	40	44	16
RAITH ROVERS,	38	30	2	6	98	28	62	14
AYR UNITED,	44	30	10	4	130	46	70	18
PORT-GLASGOW ATH.,	16	13	2	1	62	11	28	4
ST. BERNARDS,	14	11	1	2	45	21	23	5
CLYDEBANK,	14	10	3	1	39	11	23	5
ABERCORN,	8	7	1	0	33	9	15	1
LEITH ATHLETIC,	12	10	1	1	37	18	21	3
RENTON,	6	5	1	0	20	9	11	1
ALBION ROVERS,	18	15	2	1	59	18	32	4
VALE OF LEVEN,	4	4	0	0	20	2	8	0
CAMBUSLANG,	4	4	0	0	16	4	8	0
COWLAIRS,	2	1	1	0	3	1	3	1
ALLOA,	2	2	0	0	4	0	4	0
ST. JOHNSTONE,	26	19	3	4	75	26	41	11
COWDENBEATH,	20	16	2	2	68	23	34	6
DUNDEE UNITED,	8	6	0	2	19	6	12	4
DUNFERMLINE ATH.,	10	10	0	0	49	12	20	0
BO'NESS,	2	1	1	0	4	2	3	1
EAST FIFE,	8	7	1	0	25	4	15	1
EAST STIRLINGSHIRE	2	2	0	0	7	2	4	0
QUEEN OF THE S'TH,	20	16	2	2	49	15	34	6
STIRLING ALBION,	2	2	0	0	4	1	4	0
ARBROATH,	8	4	4	0	21	5	12	4
TOTALS	1708	1140	310	250	4190	1797	2590	822

SUMMARY OF LEAGUE RESULTS.

| SEASON. | Played | Won | Drawn | Lost | GOALS. | | POINTS. |
					For.	Agst	
1890-91, -	**18**	**13**	**3**	**2**	**58**	**25**	**29†**
1891-92, -	22	11	2	9	59	46	24
1892-93, -	18	12	4	2	41	27	28
1893-94, -	18	8	4	6	44	30	20
1894-95, -	18	10	2	6	41	26	22
1895-96, -	18	11	4	3	57	39	26
1896-97, -	18	11	3	4	64	30	25
1897-98, -	18	13	3	2	71	15	29
1898-99, -	**18**	**18**	**0**	**0**	**79**	**18**	**36***
1899-1900, -	**18**	**15**	**2**	**1**	**69**	**27**	**32***
1900-01, -	**20**	**17**	**1**	**2**	**60**	**25**	**35***
1901-02, -	**18**	**13**	**2**	**3**	**43**	**29**	**28***
1902-03, -	22	12	5	5	56	30	29
1903-04, -	26	16	6	4	80	33	38
1904-05, -	26	19	3	4	83	28	41‡
1905-06, -	30	15	7	8	58	48	37
1906-07, -	34	19	7	8	69	33	45
1907-08, -	34	21	8	5	74	40	50
1908-09, -	34	19	7	8	91	38	45
1909-10, -	34	20	6	8	70	35	46
1910-11, -	**34**	**23**	**6**	**5**	**90**	**34**	**52***
1911-12, -	**34**	**24**	**3**	**7**	**86**	**34**	**51***
1912-13, -	**34**	**24**	**5**	**5**	**76**	**41**	**53***
1913-14, -	38	27	5	6	79	31	59
1914-15, -	38	23	4	11	74	47	50
1915-16, -	38	25	6	7	87	39	56
1916-17, -	38	24	5	9	68	32	53
1917-18, -	**34**	**25**	**6**	**3**	**66**	**24**	**56***

* Champions.   † Joint Champions with Dumbarton.
‡ Tied for Championship with Celtic and lost the Deciding Match.

SUMMARY OF LEAGUE RESULTS—*Continued.*

SEASON.		Played.	Won.	Drawn.	Lost.	GOALS		POINTS.
						For.	Agst.	
1918-19,	-	34	26	5	3	86	16	57
1919-20,	-	42	31	9	2	106	25	71*
1920-21,	-	42	35	6	1	91	24	76*
1921-22,	-	42	28	10	4	83	26	66
1922-23,	-	38	23	9	6	67	29	55*
1923-24,	-	38	25	9	4	72	22	59*
1924-25,	-	38	25	10	3	76	26	60*
1925-26,	-	38	19	6	13	79	55	44
1926-27,	-	38	23	10	5	85	41	56*
1927-28,	-	38	26	8	4	109	36	60*
1928-29,	-	38	30	7	1	107	32	67*
1929-30,	-	38	28	4	6	84	32	60*
1930-31,	-	38	27	6	5	96	29	60*
1931-32,	-	38	28	5	5	118	42	61
1932-33,	-	38	26	10	2	113	43	62*
1933-44,	-	38	30	6	2	118	41	66*
1934-35,	-	38	25	5	8	96	46	55*
1935-86,	-	38	27	7	4	110	43	61
1936-37,	-	38	26	9	3	88	32	61*
1937-38,	-	38	18	13	7	75	49	49
1938-39,	-	38	25	9	4	112	55	59*
1946-47,	-	30	21	4	5	76	26	46*
1947-48,	-	30	21	4	5	64	28	46
1948-49,	-	30	20	6	4	63	32	46*
1949-50,	-	30	22	6	2	58	26	50*
1950-51,	-	30	17	4	9	64	37	38
Totals,	-	**1706**	**1140**	**306**	**260**	**4199**	**1797**	**2586**

* Champions.

WAR YEARS.

WEST REGIONAL LEAGUE.

| SEASON. | Played. | Won. | Drawn. | Lost. | GOALS. | | POINTS. |
					For.	Agst.	
1939-40,	30	22	4	4	72	36	48*

SOUTHERN LEAGUE.

1940-41,	30	21	4	5	79	33	46*
1941-42,	30	22	4	4	97	35	48*
1942-43,	30	22	6	2	89	23	50*
1943-44,	30	23	4	3	90	27	50*
1944-45,	30	23	3	4	88	27	49*
1945-46,	30	22	4	4	85	41	48*
Totals	**210**	**155**	**29**	**26**	**600**	**222**	**339**

* Champions.

RANGERS' LEAGUE RESULTS

1890 to 1951.

RANGERS' LEAGUE RESULTS.

CLUB.	1890-91. Home.		1890-91. Away.		1891-92. Home.		1891-92. Away.		1892-93. Home.		1892-93. Away.		1893-94. Home.		1893-94. Away.	
	F.	A.	F.	A.	F.	A.	F.	A.	F.	A.	F.	A.	F.	A.	F.	A.
Celtic, - - -	1	2	2	2	1	1	0	3	2	2	0	3	5	0	2	3
Hearts, - -	5	2	1	0	0	1	2	3	2	1	2	1	1	2	2	4
Third Lanark, -	4	1	4	0	2	3	2	2	2	1	4	2	0	3	2	1
St. Mirren, -	8	2	7	3	2	3	4	3	0	0	2	2	5	0	2	2
Dumbarton, -	4	2	1	5	1	3	0	6	3	2	0	3	4	0	0	2
Abercorn, -	2	0	1	1	6	2	1	0	4	3	4	0	..	..	..	..
Cambuslang, -	2	1	6	2	2	1	6	0	..	..	..	..	..	..	..	..
Vale of Leven, -	4	0	3	1	7	0	6	1	..	..	..	..	..	..	..	..
Cowlairs, -	1	1	2	0	..	..	..	..	..	..	..	..	..	..	..	..
Renton,* -	..	..	..	..	5	2	4	1	2	0	2	2	5	3	2	1

Table (rotated 90°). Four season summary blocks for Clyde, Leith Athletic, St. Bernards, and Dundee.

Section — "Fourth."

	P.	W.	L.	D.	GOALS F.	GOALS A.	PTS.
Clyde	..	..	..	..			
Leith Athletic	1	0	2	2			
St. Bernards	1	2	0	0			
Dundee	7	2	3	3			
Total	18	8	6	4	44	30	20

Fourth.

Section — "Second."

	P.	W.	L.	D.	GOALS F.	GOALS A.	PTS.
Clyde	4	2	3	0			
Leith Athletic	3	2	2	1			
St. Bernards	..	..	..	..			
Dundee	..	..	..	..			
Total	18	12	2	4	41	27	28

Second.

Section — "Fifth."

	P.	W.	L.	D.	GOALS F.	GOALS A.	PTS.
Clyde	1	5	3	1			
Leith Athletic	3	2	1	3			
St. Bernards	..	..	..	..			
Dundee	..	..	..	..			
Total	22	11	9	2	59	46	24

Fifth.

Section — Champions

	P.	W.	L.	D.	GOALS F.	GOALS A.	PTS.
Clyde	..	..	..	..			
Leith Athletic	..	..	..	..			
St. Bernards	..	..	..	..			
Dundee	..	..	..	..			
Total	18	13	2	3	58	25	29

Joint Champions with Dumbarton, after a deciding Match. Drawn, 2-2.

* Renton expelled for irregularity, 1890-91. Re-admitted, 1891-92.

RANGERS' LEAGUE RESULTS.

CLUB	1894-95				1895-96				1896-97				1897-98			
	Home		Away		Home		Away		Home		Away		Home		Away	
	F.	A.	F.	A.	F.	A.	F.	A.	F.	A.	F.	A.	F.	A.	F.	A.
Celtic, - - -	1	1	3	5	2	4	2	6	2	0	1	1	0	4	0	0
Hearts, - -	0	1	0	0	7	2	2	1	5	0	1	2	2	0	2	2
Third Lanark, -	0	1	2	0	0	4	3	2	6	1	1	1	0	0	3	0
St. Mirren, -	4	3	2	4	3	3	7	1	5	1	2	2	9	0	5	1
Dumbarton, -	3	0	0	1	3	1	5	3	..	..	..	..	..	..	..	..
Abercorn, - -	..	..	..	..	..	..	..	..	6	1	9	2	..	..	..	..
Clyde, - - -	4	1	5	1	4	4	2	2	2	1	7	2	7	0	8	1
Leith, - - -	5	1	4	3	..	..	..	..	..	..	..	..	..	..	..	..
St. Bernards, -	2	1	4	1	2	0	4	3	3	2	2	3	8	1	4	2
Dundee, - -	1	0	1	2	3	1	3	1	3	1	2	3	5	0	1	2

	P.	W.	L.	D.	F.	A.	PTS.	
	18	10	6	2	41	26	22	Third.
Hibernian,	..	..	..	..				
Partick Thistle,	..	..	..	..				
	18	11	3	4	57	39	26	Second.
Hibernian,	4	0	1	1				
Partick Thistle,	..	..	..	..				
	18	11	4	3	64	30	25	Third.
Hibernian,	4	3	3	4				
Partick Thistle,	..	..	..	..				
	18	13	2	3	71	15	29	Second.
Hibernian,	1	0	5	0				
Partick Thistle,	6	1	5	1				

RANGERS' LEAGUE RESULTS.

CLUB.	1898-99. Home.		Away.		1899-1900. Home.		Away.		1900-01. Home.		Away.		1901-02. Home.		Away.	
	F.	A.	F.	A.	F.	A.	F.	A.	F.	A.	F.	A.	F.	A.	F.	A.
Celtic, - - -	4	1	4	0	3	3	2	3	2	1	1	2	2	2	4	2
Hearts, - - -	3	1	3	2	4	3	1	1	1	0	1	0	2	1	2	0
Third Lanark, -	4	1	3	2	2	1	5	1	4	0	1	1	1	4	2	2
St. Mirren, - -	3	2	3	1	4	1	3	1	5	2	4	1	3	2	5	1
Clyde, - - -	8	0	3	0	7	0	6	2	..	..	..	..	..	..	..	..
St. Bernards, -	5	2	2	0	4	3	4	1	..	..	..	..	..	..	..	..
Dundee, - -	7	0	2	1	6	0	3	2	4	2	5	1	3	1	3	0
Hibernian, - -	10	0	4	3	3	2	2	0	6	0	1	4	0	2	3	2
Partick Thistle, -	6	2	5	0	..	..	..	..	4	1	2	1	..	..	..	..
Kilmarnock, - -	..	..	..	..	6	1	4	2	5	1	2	1	3	2	2	4

	P.	W.	L.	D.	PTS.		F.	A.
Morton, - - - -	..	..	..	..		**GOALS.**		
Queen's Park, - -	..	..	..	..				
	18	18	0	0	36		79	18
Champions.								

	P.	W.	L.	D.	PTS.		F.	A.
Morton,	..	..	..	..		**GOALS.**		
Queen's Park,	..	..	..	..				
	18	15	1	2	32		69	27
Champions.								

	P.	W.	L.	D.	PTS.		F.	A.
Morton,	3	2	3	1		**GOALS.**		
Queen's Park,	3	2	3	2				
	20	17	2	1	35		60	25
Champions.								

	P.	W.	L.	D.	PTS.		F.	A.
Morton,	2	1	3	2		**GOALS.**		
Queen's Park,	2	1	1	0				
	18	13	3	2	28		43	29
Champions.								

† Both games with Celtic played at Parkhead in 1899-1900. St. Mirren were played at Meadowside and Paisley. St. Bernards played both games at Ibrox.

117

RANGERS' LEAGUE RESULTS.

CLUB.	1902-03. Home		1902-03. Away		1903-04. Home		1903-04. Away		1904-05. Home		1904-05. Away		1905-06. Home		1905-06. Away	
	F.	A.	F.	A.	F.	A.	F.	A.	F.	A.	F.	A.	F.	A.	F.	A.
Celtic, - - -	3	3	1	1	0	0	2	2	1	4	2	2	3	2	0	1
Hearts, - -	2	1	1	2	5	1	1	2	1	1	5	0	0	5	2	2
Third Lanark, -	2	0	2	4	4	3	0	1	3	1	1	2	2	4	0	3
St. Mirren, -	2	2	1	0	2	2	4	5	2	3	0	3	1	0	2	3
Dundee, - -	1	1	1	3	6	1	1	3	2	1	3	0	1	1	1	1
Hibernian, -	2	5	0	1	1	1	2	1	4	0	2	1	1	1	2	1
Partick Thistle, -	9	0	4	2	2	0	4	1	8	1	4	1	1	0	1	1
Kilmarnock, -	5	0	0	0	3	0	2	2	6	2	4	0	3	2	3	1
Morton, - -	4	1	4	0	5	0	3	1	5	0	2	0	1	2	3	0
Queen's Park, -	3	2	2	0	5	0	3	2	5	0	4	0	3	1	2	1

118

Port-Glasgow Athletic,

Club	P	W	L	D	F	A	PTS.
Port-Glasgow Athletic,	4	2	3	0	..	..	..
Airdrieonians,	..	..	..	..	..	..	..
Motherwell,	..	..	..	..	..	..	..
Aberdeen,	..	..	..	..	..	..	..
Falkirk,	..	..	..	..	..	..	..
Total	22	12	5	5	56	30	29

Third.

Club	P	W	L	D	F	A	PTS.
Port-Glasgow Athletic,	8	1	1	1	..	..	..
Airdrieonians,	5	0	3	1	..	..	..
Motherwell,	3	0	5	2	..	..	..
Aberdeen,	..	..	..	..	..	..	..
Falkirk,	..	..	..	..	..	..	..
Total	26	16	4	6	80	33	38

Third.

Club	P	W	L	D	F	A	PTS.
Port-Glasgow Athletic,	5	1	3	0	..	..	..
Airdrieonians,	4	1	2	2	..	..	..
Motherwell,	3	2	2	0	..	..	..
Aberdeen,	..	..	..	..	..	..	..
Falkirk,	..	..	..	..	..	..	..
Total	26	19	4	3	83	28	41

Lost to Celtic on play-off for Championship.

Club	P	W	L	D	F	A	PTS.
Port-Glasgow Athletic,	4	0	4	1	..	..	..
Airdrieonians,	1	3	1	5	..	..	..
Motherwell,	2	1	3	3	..	..	..
Aberdeen,	1	0	1	1	..	..	..
Falkirk,	3	1	6	1	..	..	..
Total	30	15	8	7	58	48	37

Fourth.

† Both matches with Morton in 1903-04 played at Greenock, and both matches with Third Lanark at Ibrox.

RANGERS' LEAGUE RESULTS.

CLUB	1906-07 Home F.	A.	1906-07 Away F.	A.	1907-08 Home F.	A.	1907-08 Away F.	A.	1908-09 Home F.	A.	1908-09 Away F.	A.	1909-10 Home F.	A.	1909-10 Away F.	A.
Celtic,	2	1	1	2	0	1	1	2	1	3	3	2	0	0	1	1
Hearts,	1	1	1	0	2	1	2	1	4	3	0	0	1	0	3	1
Third Lanark,	0	0	2	0	2	0	5	3	2	2	0	1	1	0	1	2
St. Mirren,	1	1	0	0	2	2	2	0	1	1	3	1	1	1	6	1
Clyde,	4	0	5	1	1	1	2	0	2	2	1	0	1	0	0	1
Dundee,	2	2	0	2	2	0	2	1	2	0	0	4	2	1	2	4
Hibernian,	1	0	3	1	1	1	3	0	0	0	0	1	1	0	0	1
Partick Thistle,	1	2	2	2	3	2	2	1	2	0	6	0	2	1	0	0
Kilmarnock,	3	0	5	1	1	0	2	0	1	1	5	0	3	0	2	0
Morton,	2	0	1	2	3	0	3	2	8	0	7	1	2	1	4	1

League record — Queen's Park

Table 1 — Third. (Pts. 45)

Club	P.	W.	L.	D.
Queen's Park	3	2	2	1
Port-Glasgow Athletic	5	0	2	0
Airdrieonians	2	1	3	2
Motherwell	0	1	0	1
Aberdeen	6	2	3	0
Falkirk	2	2	1	2
Hamilton Academicals	0	1	3	0
Total	**34**	**19**	**8**	**7**

GOALS — F. 69 A. 33 PTS. 45 Third.

Table 2 — Third. (Pts. 50)

Club	P.	W.	L.	D.
Queen's Park	1	1	1	3
Port-Glasgow Athletic	5	1	6	1
Airdrieonians	1	2	0	3
Motherwell	4	2	2	1
Aberdeen	4	0	0	0
Falkirk	2	2	4	4
Hamilton Academicals	1	0	2	2
Total	**34**	**21**	**5**	**8**

GOALS — F. 74 A. 40 PTS. 50 Third.

Table 3 — Fourth. (Pts. 45)

Club	P.	W.	L.	D.
Queen's Park	2	3	1	1
Port-Glasgow Athletic	7	0	0	2
Airdrieonians	2	0	3	4
Motherwell	3	1	5	2
Aberdeen	3	1	2	0
Falkirk	4	1	0	1
Hamilton Academicals	4	0	7	0
Total	**34**	**19**	**8**	**7**

GOALS — F. 91 A. 38 PTS. 45 Fourth.

Table 4 — Third. (Pts. 46)

Club	P.	W.	L.	D.
Queen's Park	7	1	2	3
Port-Glasgow Athletic	4	0	1	1
Airdrieonians	3	0	1	2
Motherwell	4	1	3	2
Aberdeen	2	1	1	1
Falkirk	0	1	1	3
Hamilton Academicals	5	1	3	2
Total	**34**	**20**	**8**	**6**

GOALS — F. 70 A. 35 PTS. 46 Third.

† In seasons 1908-09 and 1910-11 Partick Thistle played both matches at Ibrox.

RANGERS' LEAGUE RESULTS.

CLUB.	1910-11. Home F.	A.	Away F.	A.	1911-12. Home F.	A.	Away F.	A.	1912-13. Home F.	A.	Away F.	A.	1913-14. Home F.	A.	Away F.	A.
Celtic, - - -	1	1	1	0	3	1	0	3	0	1	2	3	0	2	0	4
Hearts, - - -	2	0	4	1	2	1	1	2	2	4	1	1	3	2	1	2
Third Lanark, - -	3	1	1	1	4	0	3	1	2	1	1	0	2	0	4	2
St. Mirren, - -	1	0	1	2	4	0	5	1	2	1	3	0	2	1	1	0
Dumbarton, - -	..	..	..	..	..	..	..	..	..	..	..	..	3	2	3	0
Clyde, - - -	6	1	1	0	1	2	2	0	3	1	1	0	2	1	1	0
Dundee, - -	1	2	2	0	2	1	1	2	3	3	0	0	0	1	2	0
Hibernian, - -	4	0	3	1	2	0	0	5	5	3	1	0	1	1	3	0
Partick Thistle, -	2	2	2	0	4	1	1	0	2	0	3	2	0	0	1	1
Kilmarnock, - -	3	0	2	0	6	1	2	3	3	0	3	2	1	0	6	1

	P	W	L	D	P	W	L	D	P	W	L	D	P	W	L	D
Morton,	1	5	2	2	6	1	1	2	1	1	3	0	1	0	1	0
Queen's Park,	4	0	4	0	1	0	0	0	4	0	3	2	3	0	6	0
Airdrieonians,	7	1	4	1	4	1	2	2	4	2	0	3	2	0	3	0
Motherwell,	7	1	2	1	3	1	2	1	3	1	2	1	0	0	0	1
Aberdeen,	2	4	0	1	2	0	2	1	3	1	3	1	5	1	0	0
Falkirk,	1	1	2	2	4	0	2	0	2	1	0	2	3	0	1	4
Hamilton Academicals,	4	0	4	2	7	0	1	1	3	2	2	0	3	0	1	0
Raith Rovers,	4	1	2	0	5	0	1	0	4	0	2	2	4	0	3	0
Ayr United,	.	.	.	.	.	.	.	.	.	.	.	.	5	2	2	1
	P.	W.	L.	D.	P.	W.	L.	D.	P.	W.	L.	D.	P.	W.	L.	D.
	34	23	5	6	34	24	7	3	34	24	5	5	38	27	6	5

	GOALS.		PTS.	GOALS.		PTS.	GOALS.		PTS.	GOALS.		PTS.
	F.	A.		F.	A.		F.	A.		F.	A.	
	90	34	52	86	34	51	76	41	53	79	31	59
	Champions.			Champions.			Champions.			Second.		

RANGERS' LEAGUE RESULTS.

CLUB.	1914-15. Home.		Away.		1915-16. Home.		Away.		1916-17. Home.		Away.		1917-18. Home.		Away.	
	F.	A.	F.	A.	F.	A.	F.	A.	F.	A.	F.	A.	F.	A.	F.	A.
Celtic, - - -	2	1	1	2	3	0	2	2	0	0	0	0	1	2	0	0
Hearts, - - -	1	2	4	3	0	4	2	1	1	0	3	1	2	0	3	0
Third Lanark, -	3	0	1	1	4	0	1	0	0	2	1	1	4	2	1	0
St. Mirren, -	5	0	2	0	4	0	1	1	1	0	1	1	2	0	0	0
Dumbarton, -	1	0	1	1	2	2	3	1	6	0	3	0	2	1	4	2
Clyde, - -	1	2	2	1	2	2	2	0	1	0	1	0	2	1	3	0
Dundee, -	2	0	1	1	3	2	0	2	3	1	1	2	..	..	..	..
Hibernian, -	4	2	2	3	4	2	3	2	5	1	0	0	3	0	1	0
Partick Thistle, -	0	1	1	0	0	1	2	5	3	0	1	0	1	0	0	2
Kilmarnock, -	2	1	1	0	3	1	3	0	3	0	1	4	3	0	1	0
Morton, - -	0	2	1	0	1	0	0	2	0	1	0	1	4	2	1	1
Queen's Park, -	4	1	4	0	6	0	6	0	1	0	4	1	3	0	3	2

Club	P.	W.	L.	D.	P.	W.	L.	D.	P.	W.	L.	D.	P.	W.	L.	D.
Airdrieonians	0	5	2	1	3	0	1	0	3	0	0	2	4	0	2	1
Motherwell	5	0	4	2	4	1	2	2	2	1	1	2	2	1	0	0
Aberdeen	1	1	2	0	4	0	0	0	1	0	1	3	··	··	··	··
Falkirk	3	0	3	1	1	0	0	2	3	1	2	0	4	1	0	2
Hamilton Academicals	1	0	3	4	3	0	1	0	2	0	1	3	4	2	2	1
Raith Rovers	1	2	2	1	3	0	3	1	4	3	4	1	··	··	··	··
Ayr United	1	3	0	2	5	2	0	1	1	0	3	1	0	0	2	0
Clydebank	··	··	··	··	··	··	··	··	··	··	··	··	1	0	1	1

	P.	W.	L.	D.	GOALS F.	A.	PTS.	
Totals	38	23	11	4	74	47	50	Third.
Totals	38	25	7	6	87	39	56	Second.
Totals	38	24	9	5	68	32	53	Third.
Totals	34	25	3	6	66	24	56	Champions.

† Season 1914-15, Clyde played both matches at Ibrox.

RANGERS' LEAGUE RESULTS.

CLUB.	1918-19 Home F.	A.	Away F.	A.	1919-20 Home F.	A.	Away F.	A.	1920-21 Home F.	A.	Away F.†	A.	1921-22 Home F.	A.	Away F.	A.
Celtic,	1	1	3	0	3	0	1	1	0	2	2	1	1	1	0	0
Hearts,	3	2	4	1	3	0	0	0	0	0	4	0	0	2	2	1
Third Lanark,	4	0	2	1	6	1	2	0	2	1	1	0	2	1	3	1
St. Mirren,	2	0	2	2	3	1	4	0	2	0	1	0	4	1	2	1
Dumbarton,	3	0	2	0	4	0	0	0	2	0	5	2	1	1	4	0
Clyde,	3	0	4	0	1	0	0	0	3	1	3	1	3	0	0	0
Dundee,	..	..	..	..	6	1	2	0	5	0	2	1	2	1	0	0
Hibernian,	5	1	2	1	7	0	1	1	1	0	1	1	2	0	0	0
Partick Thistle,	2	0	0	1	2	2	2	1	3	0	2	0	2	2	1	0
Kilmarnock,	8	0	0	1	5	0	7	1	2	0	2	1	1	0	2	1
Morton,	1	0	0	1	3	1	2	0	2	0	0	0	3	0	2	1
Queen's Park,	4	0	2	0	3	1	0.	0	3	1	1	1	2	1	4	2

Table 1 (Second)

	P.	W.	L.	D.
Airdrieonians	2	1	0	1
Motherwell	0	0	1	0
Aberdeen	..	..	..	..
Falkirk	1	0	4	0
Hamilton Academicals	3	0	3	0
Raith Rovers	..	..	..	..
Ayr United	6	2	1	1
Clydebank	3	0	5	0
Albion Rovers	..	..	..	..
Totals	34	26	3	5

GOALS — F. 86, A. 16. PTS. 57. Second.

Table 2 (Champions)

	P.	W.	L.	D.
Airdrieonians	3	2	1	0
Motherwell	0	0	0	1
Aberdeen	3	2	2	0
Falkirk	3	1	3	0
Hamilton Academicals	4	1	2	1
Raith Rovers	3	2	2	1
Ayr United	2	1	3	0
Clydebank	1	2	0	†0
Albion Rovers	3	0	4	0
Totals	42	31	2	9

GOALS — F. 106, A. 25. PTS. 71. Champions.

Table 3 (Champions)

	P.	W.	L.	D.
Airdrieonians	4	1	3	0
Motherwell	2	1	2	0
Aberdeen	2	1	1	1
Falkirk	2	0	2	0
Hamilton Academicals	4	0	1	0
Raith Rovers	1	0	1	0
Ayr United	7	2	1	1
Clydebank	1	0	4	2
Albion Rovers	2	1	2	1
Totals	42	35	1	6

GOALS — F. 91, A. 24. PTS. 76. Champions.

Table 4 (Second)

	P.	W.	L.	D.
Airdrieonians	3	0	2	1
Motherwell	2	1	0	2
Aberdeen	1	0	0	0
Falkirk	0	0	0	1
Hamilton Academicals	5	0	0	0
Raith Rovers	0	1	3	0
Ayr United	2	0	1	0
Clydebank	6	1	7	1
Albion Rovers	3	1	5	0
Totals	42	28	4	10

GOALS — F. 83, A. 26. PTS. 66. Second.

† Third Lanark were played away at Hampden, also St. Mirren.

RANGERS' LEAGUE RESULTS.

CLUB.	1922-23 Home		1922-23 Away		1923-24 Home		1923-24 Away		1924-25 Home		1924-25 Away		1925-26 Home		1925-26 Away	
	F.	A.	F.	A.	F.	A.	F.	A.	F.	A.	F.	A.	F.	A.	F.	A.
Celtic, - - -	2	0	3	1	0	0	2	2	4	1	1	0	1	0	2	2
Hearts, - - -	3	0	0	0	1	0	0	0	4	1	2	1	2	2	0	3
Third Lanark, -	5	1	2	2	2	0	3	1	5	2	1	1	..	..	..	..
St. Mirren, -	1	1	0	1	5	0	0	0	3	1	4	1	4	1	2	3
Clyde, - - -	2	1	2	1	2	1	1	3	..	..	..	..	..	..	..	..
Dundee, - -	4	1	2	1	1	1	4	1	2	0	0	0	1	2	5	1
Hibernian, - -	2	0	0	2	2	1	3	1	3	0	1	4	3	1	2	0
Partick Thistle, -	4	1	1	0	1	0	6	0	4	0	1	0	2	1	0	2
Kilmarnock, -	1	0	2	1	2	0	1	1	1	1	0	0	3	0	2	2
Morton, - -	0	0	1	1	2	1	1	0	2	0	1	1	4	1	3	1
Queen's Park, -	..	..	..	..	1	0	2	0	1	1	3	1	1	2	6	3.
Airdrieonians, -	4	1	0	1	0	0	0	0	1	1	0	1	1	2	1	2
Motherwell, -	2	1	4	0	3	0	3	3	1	0	1	1	1	0	3	1

	Champions.				Champions.				Champions.				Sixth.			
	P.	W.	L.	D.	P.	W.	L.	D.	P.	W.	L.	D.	P.	W.	L.	D.
Aberdeen,	1	1	0	0	2	0	0	1	2	0	1	0	0	1	1	3
Falkirk,	2	0	0	2	2	2	1	0	3	1	1	1	2	3	1	1
Hamilton Academicals,	3	0	3	0	4	0	3	2	2	0	0	1	2	0	3	3
Raith Rovers,	1	0	0	2	0	1	1	0	3	0	4	0	4	2	0	1
Ayr United,	2	1	1	1	5	0	1	2	1	0	4	0	..	..	..	..
Clydebank,	..	..	..	..	3	0	2	1	..	..	..	..	3	1	2	2
Albion Rovers,	2	2	1	2	..	..	..	..	..	..	..	..	..	..	..	..
Alloa Athletic,	2	0	2	0	..	..	..	..	..	..	..	..	..	..	..	..
St. Johnstone,	..	..	..	..	..	..	..	..	3	1	3	1	0	1	3	0
Cowdenbeath,	..	..	..	..	..	..	..	..	1	0	2	2	3	0	3	2
Dundee United,	..	..	..	..	..	..	..	..	..	..	..	..	2	1	1	2
Totals	38	23	6	9	38	25	4	9	38	25	3	10	38	19	13	6

	GOALS F.	GOALS A.	PTS.
Champions.	67	29	55
Champions.	72	22	59
Champions.	76	26	60
Sixth.	79	55	44

RANGERS' LEAGUE RESULTS.

CLUB.	1926-27 Home		1926-27 Away		1927-28 Home		1927-28 Away		1928-29 Home		1928-29 Away		1929-30 Home		1929-30 Away	
	F.	A.	F.	A.	F.	A.	F.	A.	F.	A.	F.	A.	F.	A.	F.	A.
Celtic, - - - -	2	1	1	0	1	0	0	1	3	0	2	1	1	0	2	1
Hearts, - - -	1	0	2	0	4	1	0	0	2	0	1	0	1	3	0	2
Third Lanark, -	:			:	.		.	.	5	1	5	2	:	:		:
St. Mirren, - -	4	0	7	3	4	2	3	3	1	1	5	1	2	1	1	0
Clyde, - - -	6	0	0	0	3	1	4	3	0	0	3	2	3	0	3	3
Dundee, - -	0	0	1	1	5	1	1	0	3	0	3	2	4	1	3	1
Hibernian, - -	2	0	2	2	4	1	1	2	3	0	2	1	3	0	2	0
Partick Thistle, -	2	1	4	1	2	1	6	0	1	0	1	1	2	1	1	1
Kilmarnock, - -	1	0	0	0	5	1	1	1	4	2	3	1	4	0	0	1
Morton, - -	2	1	8	2	.	.	.	.	.	.	.	.	3	0	2	2
Queen's Park, -	0	1	2	1	4	0	1	3	2	1	4	0	1	0	3	1
Airdrieonians, -	1	1	3	3	2	1	7	2	2	0	5	2	2	0	0	1
Motherwell, -	2	0	4	1	0	2	1	1	0	0	4	2	4	2	2	0

	Group 1				Group 2				Group 3				Group 4			
	D.	L.	W.	P.	D.	L.	W.	P.	D.	L.	W.	P.	D.	L.	W.	P.
Aberdeen,	1	1	1	3	2	2	0	2	2	3	0	5	2	2	2	3
Falkirk,	2	1	0	4	1	4	1	1	1	2	0	4	3	3	1	2
Hamilton Academicals,	1	1	2	5	3	1	0	4	1	1	1	3	1	1	4	1
Raith Rovers,	:	:	:	:	1	3	1	7	0	0	0	7	:	:	:	:
Ayr United,	0	3	0	9	1	3	0	0	:	:	:	:	:	:	:	:
St. Johnstone,	0	1	1	6	1	3	0	8	0	1	1	5	2	1	2	4
Cowdenbeath,	3	2	0	5	0	2	1	3	1	4	2	2	1	0	1	4
Dundee United,	0	1	1	3	:	:	:	:	:	:	:	:	2	0	0	2
Dunfermline, -	:	:	:	:	:	:	:	:	0	5	0	4	1	3	0	2
Bo'ness,	:	:	:	:	:	:	:	:	1	1	1	3	:	:	:	:
	D. 4	L. 6	W. 28	P. 38	D. 7	L. 1	W. 30	P. 38	D. 8	L. 4	W. 26	P. 38	D. 10	L. 5	W. 23	P. 38
GOALS	F. 94	A. 32			F. 107	A. 32			F. 109	A. 36			F. 85	A. 41		
PTS.	60				67				60				56			
	Champions.				Champions.				Champions.				Champions.			

RANGERS' LEAGUE RESULTS.

CLUB.	1930-31 Home F.	A.	1930-31 Away F.	A.	1931-32 Home F.	A.	1931-32 Away F.	A.	1932-33 Home F.	A.	1932-33 Away F.	A.	1933-34 Home F.	A.	1933-34 Away F.	A.
Celtic,	1	0	0	2	0	0	2	1	0	0	1	1	2	2	2	2
Hearts,	4	1	0	3	4	2	0	0	4	4	0	1	3	1	2	1
Third Lanark,	..	..	..	..	6	1	3	4	5	0	3	1	1	0	1	0
St. Mirren,	1	1	1	1	4	0	2	0	4	0	0	2	3	0	2	1
Clyde,	5	1	8	0	2	2	1	0	2	2	5	0	3	1	6	1
Leith Athletic,	4	1	3	1	4	0	5	1	..	..	..	..	..	..	..	..
Dundee,	3	0	1	0	4	1	2	2	6	4	3	0	1	0	6	0
Hibernian,	1	0	2	1	..	..	..	..	..	..	..	..	6	0	0	0
Partick Thistle,	3	1	1	1	4	0	3	1	3	0	0	0	2	2	4	3
Kilmarnock,	1	0	0	1	3	0	4	2	2	0	6	2	2	2	3	1
Morton,	7	1	2	1	7	3	2	1	6	1	3	1	..	..	..	..
Queen's Park,	2	0	2	0	0	1	6	1	1	0	0	0	4	0	1	1
Airdrieonians,	0	1	3	3	2	1	0	3	5	1	2	1	5	1	7	2

Team	P	W	L	D	P	W	L	D	P	W	L	D	P	W	L	D
Motherwell	4	1	0	1	1	0	2	4	2	2	3	1	4	2	1	2
Aberdeen	1	0	3	1	4	1	0	0	3	1	1	1	2	1	2	1
Falkirk	1	0	3	1	4	0	2	1	5	1	4	1	3	1	3	1
Hamilton Academicals	1	0	3	0	1	0	2	1	4	4	4	2	4	2	2	1
Ayr United	5	1	2	2	6	1	3	1	4	1	3	3	9	1	2	0
St. Johnstone	..	..	..	..	..	..	..	..	3	0	2	0	3	0	1	3
Cowdenbeath	7	0	3	1	6	1	7	1	4	1	3	2	3	1	4	3
Dundee United	..	..	..	..	5	0	5	0	..	..	..	..	..	..	..	..
East Fife	4	0	4	0	..	..	..	..	..	..	..	..	..	..	..	..
East Stirling	..	..	..	..	..	..	..	..	4	0	3	2	..	..	..	..
Queen of the South	..	..	..	..	..	..	..	..	..	..	..	..	5	1	4	0
P. W. L. D.	38	27	5	6	38	28	5	5	38	26	2	10	38	30	2	6
GOALS F.	96				118				113				118			
GOALS A.	29				42				43				41			
PTS.	60				61				62				66			
	Champions.				Second.				Champions.				Champions.			

RANGERS' LEAGUE RESULTS.

CLUB.	1934-35 Home		Away		1935-36 Home		Away		1936-37 Home		Away		1937-38 Home		Away	
	F.	A.	F.	A.	F.	A.	F.	A.	F.	A.	F.	A.	F.	A.	F.	A.
Celtic, - - -	2	1	1	1	1	2	4	3	1	0	1	1	3	1	0	3
Hearts, - - -	2	1	1	4	1	1	1	1	0	1	2	5	0	3	2	3
Hamilton Academicals,	1	1	1	2	3	1	0	1	4	0	5	1	2	2	2	2
St. Johnstone, -	3	1	0	2	7	0	2	1	0	0	2	1	2	2	5	1
Aberdeen, - -	2	2	3	1	2	3	0	1	2	1	1	1	2	2	3	0
Motherwell, - -	1	0	2	2	0	0	2	0	3	2	4	1	2	1	1	1
Dundee, - -	3	1	2	3	4	3	3	0	3	0	0	0	6	0	1	6
Kilmarnock, -	2	3	3	1	2	1	3	0	8	0	2	1	4	1	1	2
Clyde, - -	4	2	1	2	4	1	4	1	2	0	2	3	1	0	1	1
Hibernian, - -	4	2	2	1	3	0	1	1	4	0	4	1	2	0	0	0
Queen's Park, -	0	1	4	0	3	3	3	1	1	1	1	1	2	1	3	0
Partick Thistle, -	4	0	0	1	3	1	3	1	3	1	1	0	1	3	1	1

Team	D	L	W	P	D	L	W	P	D	L	W	P	D	L	W	P
Airdrieonians,	··	··	··	··	··	··	··	··	0	2	3	5	1	2	1	3
Dunfermline Athletic,	··	··	··	··	2	3	3	5	2	6	2	6	1	7	1	8
Albion Rovers,	··	··	··	··	2	3	0	1	1	2	1	5	1	5	2	2
Queen of the South,	0	2	3	2	0	1	1	1	0	2	1	2	2	3	0	5
Ayr United,	1	1	2	2	··	··	··	··	2	2	1	6	2	4	0	2
St. Mirren,	1	1	0	4	1	4	0	2	··	··	··	··	0	2	0	1
Falkirk, -	0	1	0	0	0	2	0	3	··	··	··	··	0	3	0	1
Arbroath,	1	1	1	3	0	4	0	0	0	0	0	6	··	··	··	··
Third Lanark,	1	2	0	3	0	0	1	3	1	3	2	4	··	··	··	··
Morton, -	2	3	1	3	··	··	··	··	··	··	··	··	··	··	··	··
	13	**7**	**18**	**38**	**9**	**3**	**26**	**38**	**7**	**4**	**27**	**38**	**5**	**8**	**25**	**38**

GOALS — A. 49, F. 75; PTS. 49; **Third.**

GOALS — A. 32, F. 88; PTS. 61; **Champions.**

GOALS — A. 43, F. 110; PTS. 61; **Second.**

GOALS — A. 46, F. 96; PTS. 55; **Champions.**

RANGERS' LEAGUE RESULTS.

CLUB.	1938-39. Home.		Away.		1939-40. * Home.		Away.		1940-41. † Home.		Away.		1941-42. † Home.		Away.	
	F.	A.	F.	A.	F.	A.	F.	A.	F.	A.	F.	A.	F.	A.	F.	A.
Celtic, - - -	2	1	2	6	1	1	2	1	2	3	0	0	3	0	2	0
Aberdeen, - -	5	2	0	2	..	..	..	..	..	..	..	..	..	..	..	..
Hearts, - -	1	1	3	1	..	..	..	..	3	0	1	1	5	2	1	0
Falkirk, - -	2	1	2	2	..	..	..	..	4	0	3	1	5	2	2	2
Queen of the South,	4	1	1	1	5	1	2	1	..	..	..	..	..	..	..	..
Hamilton Academicals,	3	2	1	2	2	2	0	2	2	0	4	1	6	0	3	2
St. Johnstone, -	4	2	3	3	..	..	..	..	..	..	..	..	..	..	..	..
Clyde, - -	2	0	1	1	3	1	1	0	3	2	3	0	0	0	8	2
Kilmarnock, -	2	2	1	3	4	1	1	3	..	..	..	..	..	..	..	..
Partick Thistle, -	4	1	4	2	2	2	3	1	3	1	4	1	6	0	3	2
Motherwell, -	2	2	5	0	1	2	1	0	2	3	3	2	3	0	1	1
Hibernian, -	5	2	1	1	..	..	..	..	5	1	0	1	0	1	1	8
Ayr United, -	4	1	4	3	3	1	2	0			..	..	..	..	..	..

Scottish League Tables

Table 1 — †Southern League Champions.

	D.	L.	W.	P.
Third Lanark,	0	2	1	6
Albion Rovers,	0	1	1	2
Arbroath,	..	..	..	..
St. Mirren,	3	1	1	8
Queen's Park,	1	2	0	3
Raith Rovers,	..	..	..	..
Dunfermline Athletic,	..	..	..	..
Morton,	2	1	0	3
Airdrieonians,	1	6	0	3
Dumbarton,	3	3	0	7
Totals	D. 4	L. 4	W. 22	P. 30

GOALS — F. 97, A. 35. PTS. 48.

Table 2 — †Southern League Champions.

	D.	L.	W.	P.
Third Lanark,	0	1	3	0
Albion Rovers,	2	7	0	2
Arbroath,	..	..	.	..
St. Mirren,	2	0	0	3
Queen's Park,	0	5	1	1
Raith Rovers,	..	..	..	..
Dunfermline Athletic,	..	..	..	..
Morton,	2	4	4	5
Airdrieonians,	0	2	0	2
Dumbarton,	1	4	1	1
Totals	D. 4	L. 5	W. 21	P. 30

GOALS — F. 79, A. 33. PTS. 46.

Table 3 — *Regional League Western Division Champions.

	D.	L.	W.	P.
Third Lanark,	0	1	0	6
Albion Rovers,	3	3	1	2
Arbroath,	..	..	..	..
St. Mirren,	4	6	0	4
Queen's Park,	2	3	0	4
Raith Rovers,	..	..	..	..
Dunfermline Athletic,	..	..	..	..
Morton,	3	0	0	1
Airdrieonians,	0	1	1	3
Dumbarton,	2	3	1	2
Totals	D. 4	L. 4	W. 22	P. 30

GOALS — F. 72, A. 36. PTS. 48.

Table 4 — Champions.

	D.	L.	W.	P.
Third Lanark,	1	2	1	5
Albion Rovers,	2	7	0	5
Arbroath,	3	3	0	4
St. Mirren,	1	5	0	3
Queen's Park,	2	3	0	1
Raith Rovers,	0	2	0	4
Dunfermline Athletic,	..	..	..	..
Morton,	..	..	..	..
Airdrieonians,	..	..	..	..
Dumbarton,	..	..	..	..
Totals	D. 9	L. 4	W. 25	P. 38

GOALS — F. 112, A. 55. PTS. 59.

RANGERS' LEAGUE RESULTS.

CLUB.	1942-43. Home. F.	1942-43. Home. A.	1942-43. Away. F.	1942-43. Away. A.	1943-44. Home. F.	1943-44. Home. A.	1943-44. Away. F.	1943-44. Away. A.	1944-45. Home. F.	1944-45. Home. A.	1944-45. Away. F.	1944-45. Away. A.	1945-46. Home. F.	1945-46. Home. A.	1945-46. Away. F.	1945-46. Away. A.
Morton, - - -	7	0	1	1	4	1	1	1	2	4	4	1	4	4	2	2
Hibernian, - -	1	1	1	1	4	0	4	3	5	0	1	4	3	2	1	2
Clyde, - -	0	1	3	1	3	2	3	0	3	0	2	0	3	1	1	0
Motherwell, - -	2	1	2	0	2	0	5	0	1	1	4	0	0	3	2	1
Hamilton, - -	4	2	3	0	6	0	4	1	2	0	4	2	5	1	4	1
Hearts, - -	1	1	3	0	1	3	3	1	4	0	1	1	1	1	0	2
Falkirk, - -	1	1	5	1	2	0	2	0	4	0	3	2	1	0	3	0
Dumbarton, - -	1	0	2	2	2	0	1	1	5	2	6	3	..	..	..	..
Celtic, - -	8	1	2	0	0	1	3	1	0	1	4	0	5	3	1	0
Partick Thistle, -	4	1	2	0	3	3	2	1	2	0	4	1	4	2	5	1

Table 1

	P.	W.	L.	D.
St. Mirren,	5	0	1	0
Third Lanark,	4	2	3	0
Queen's Park,	5	2	0	1
Airdrieonians,	4	1	7	1
Albion Rovers,	3	0	4	0
Aberdeen,	..	..	..	..
Queen of the South,	..	..	..	..
Kilmarnock,	..	..	..	..
	P. 30	W. 22	L. 2	D. 6

GOALS. F. 89 A. 22 PTS. 50 †Southern League Champions.

Table 2

	P.	W.	L.	D.
St. Mirren,	1	2	4	1
Third Lanark,	3	1	6	0
Queen's Park,	1	1	4	1
Airdrieonians,	3	0	3	1
Albion Rovers,	5	0	5	1
Aberdeen,	..	..	..	..
Queen of the South,	..	..	..	..
Kilmarnock,	..	..	..	..
	P. 30	W. 23	L. 3	D. 4

GOALS. F. 90 A. 27 PTS. 50 †Southern League Champions.

Table 3

	P.	W.	L.	D.
St. Mirren,	6	1	1	0
Third Lanark,	0	0	4	1
Queen's Park,	0	1	4	1
Airdrieonians,	2	0	3	1
Albion Rovers,	3	0	4	0
Aberdeen,	..	..	..	..
Queen of the South,	..	..	..	..
Kilmarnock,	..	..	..	..
	P. 30	W. 23	L. 4	D. 3

GOALS. F. 88 A. 27 PTS. 49 †Southern League Champions.

Table 4

	P.	W.	L.	D.
St. Mirren,	3	1	2	2
Third Lanark,	1	0	5	1
Queen's Park,	2	1	2	0
Airdrieonians,	..	..	..	..
Albion Rovers,	..	..	..	..
Aberdeen,	3	1	1	4
Queen of the South,	5	2	4	2
Kilmarnock,	5	1	7	0
	P. 30	W. 22	L. 4	D. 4

GOALS. F. 85 A. 41 PTS. 48 †Southern League Champions.

RANGERS' LEAGUE RESULTS.

CLUB.	1946-47 Home F.	A.	Away F.	A.	1947-48 Home F.	A.	Away F.	A.	1948-49 Home F.	A.	Away F.	A.	1949-50 Home F.	A.	Away F.	A.
Hibernian, -	1	2	1	1	2	1	0	1	2	4	1	0	0	0	0	1
Aberdeen, -	1	0	0	1	4	0	1	1	1	1	2	0	2	2	3	1
Hearts, - -	1	2	3	0	1	2	2	1	2	1	0	2	1	0	1	1
Partick Thistle, -	4	0	2	3	2	1	1	0	2	2	1	1	2	0	3	1
Morton, - -	2	1	1	0	1	1	1	0	4	1	1	0	..	..	..	..
Celtic, - -	1	1	3	2	2	0	4	0	4	0	1	0	4	0	1	1
Motherwell, -	2	1	4	2	2	0	1	1	2	0	1	1	2	0	0	4
Third Lanark, -	8	1	1	1	5	2	1	0	2	1	1	2	3	1	2	2
Clyde, - -	5	0	4	2	2	1	2	1	4	1	3	1	5	4	2	1
Queen of the South, -	2	1	2	0	2	3	3	0	3	0	2	0	1	0	2	1
Falkirk, - -	2	1	5	0	1	1	5	1	4	3	2	2	3	0	2	0
Queen's Park, -	2	0	0	0	1	2	4	1	..	..	..	..	..	..	..	..

Team		P	W	L	D	F	A	PTS	
St. Mirren,	-	30	22	2	6	58	26	50	Champions.
Kilmarnock,	-	30	20	4	6	63	32	46	Champions.
Hamilton Academicals,	-	30	21	5	4	64	28	46	Second.
Dundee,	-	30	21	5	4	76	26	46	Champions.
Airdrieonians,	-								
East Fife,	-								
Albion Rovers,	-								
Raith Rovers,	-								
Stirling Albion,	-								

RANGERS' LEAGUE RESULTS.

CLUB.	1950-51.			
	Home.		Away.	
	F.	A.	F.	A.
Hibernian, - - -	1	1	1	4
Aberdeen, - - -	1	2	4	2
Dundee, - - - -	0	0	0	2
Hearts, - - - -	2	1	1	0
Raith Rovers, - -	4	1	1	3
Partick Thistle, - -	1	3	1	2
Celtic, - - - -	1	0	2	3
Motherwell, - - -	3	0	3	2
Third Lanark, - -	2	1	5	1
Morton, - -' - -	2	0	2	0
Clyde, - - - -	4	0	1	2
East Fife, - - -	5	0	3	0
Airdrieonians, - -	4	1	1	2
St. Mirren, - - -	1	1	2	0
Falkirk, - - - -	5	2	1	1

P.	W.	L.	D.
30	17	9	4

GOALS.		PTS.
F	A.	
64	37	38

Second.

FINISHING POSITION IN LEAGUE

1890 to 1951

FINISHING POSITION IN LEAGUE, 1890 to 1951.

Champions.	Second.	Third.	Fourth.	Fifth.	Sixth.
1890-91.*	1892-93.	1894-95.	1893-94.	1891-92.	1925-26.
1898-99	1895-96.	1896-97.	1905-06.	—	—
1899-1900	1897-98.	1902-03.	1908-09.	—	—
1900-01.	1904-05.†	1903-04	—	—	—
1901-02.	1913-14.	1906-07.	—	—	—
1910-11.	1915-16.	1907-08.	—	—	—
1911-12.	1918-19.	1909-10	—	—	—
1912-13.	1921-22.	1914-15.	—	—	—
1917-18.	1931-32.	1916-17.	—	—	—
1919-20	1935-36.	1937-38.	—	—	—
1920-21.	1947-48.	—	—	—	—
1922-23.	1950-51.	—	—	—	—

1923-24.
1924-25.
1926-27
1927-28.
1928-29.
1929-30.
1930-31.
1932-33.
1933-34
1934-35.
1936-37.
1938-39.
1946-47.
1948-49.
1949-50

* Joint Champions with Dumbarton.
† Lost to Celtic after play-off for Championship.
War Regional League, 1940—Champions.
Southern League, 1941-42-43-44-45-46—Champions.

DIRECTORS.

1934-35—Ex-Bailie Duncan Graham, J.P., O.B.E. (*Chairman*) ; James Bowie ; R. G. Campbell , Alan L. Morton.
  Mr. Graham died 15th November, 1934.

1935-36—James Bowie (*Chairman*) ; R. G. Campbell ; Alan L Morton.

1936-37—James Bowie (*Chairman*) ; R. G. Campbell ; Alan L. Morton.

1937-38—James Bowie (*Chairman*) ; R. G. Campbell ; Alan L. Morton.

1938-39—James Bowie, J.P. (*Chairman*) ; R. G. Campbell ; Alan L. Morton.

1939-40—James Bowie, J.P. (*Chairman*) ; R. G. Campbell ; Alan L. Morton.

1940-41—James Bowie, J.P. (*Chairman*) ; R. G. Campbell ; Alan L. Morton.

1941-42—James Bowie, J.P. (*Chairman*) ; R. G. Campbell ; Alan L. Morton.

1942-43—James Bowie, J.P. (*Chairman*) ; Alan L. Morton ; G. C. P. Brown.
  Mr. Campbell died 31st May, 1943.

1943-44—James Bowie, J.P. (*Chairman*) ; Alan L. Morton ; G. C. P. Brown.

1944-45—James Bowie, J.P. (*Chairman*) ; Alan L. Morton ; G. C. P. Brown

1945-46—James Bowie, J.P. (*Chairman*) ; Alan L. Morton ; G. C. P. Brown.

1946-47—James Bowie, J.P. (*Chairman*) ; Alan L. Morton ; G. C. P. Brown, M.A.

1947-48—W. R. Simpson, C.A. (*Chairman*) ; Councillor J. F. Wilson, D.L., J.P. (*Vice-Chairman*) ; Alan L. Morton ; G. C. P. Brown, M.A. ; Wm. Struth, J.P.

1948-49—W. R. Simpson, C.A. (*Chairman*) ; Councillor· J. F. Wilson, D.L., J.P. (*Vice-Chairman*) ; Alan L. Morton ; G. C. P. Brown, M.A. ; Wm. Struth, J.P.
Mr. Simpson died 29th April, 1949.

1949-50—Councillor J. F. Wilson, D.L., J.P. (*Chairman*); Wm Struth, J.P. (*Vice-Chairman*) ; Alan L. Morton ; G. C. P. Brown, M.A. ; Ex-Bailie W. Gordon Bennett.

1950-51—Councillor J. F. Wilson, D.L., J.P. (*Chairman*) ; Wm. Struth, J.P. (*Vice-Chairman*) ; Alan L. Morton ; G. C. P. Brown, M.A. ; W. Gordon Bennett, M.P.

1951-52—Councillor J. F. Wilson, D.L. J.P. (*Chairman*) ; Wm. Struth, J.P. (*Vice-Chairman*) ; Alan L. Morton ; G. C. P. Brown, M.A. ; W. Gordon Bennett, M.P.

Mr. W. Gordon Bennett resigned from the Board on Tuesday, 4th September, 1951.